Glory to God

Music Edition

PUBLISHED BY
OXFORD UNIVERSITY PRESS
ON BEHALF OF THE
PRESBYTERIAN CHURCH IN IRELAND

Oxford University Press, Walton Street, Oxford OX2 6DP

Oxford New York Toronto
Delhi Bombay Calcutta Madras Karachi
Kuala Lumpur Singapore Hong Kong Tokyo
Nairobi Dar es Salaam Cape Town
Melbourne Auckland Madrid

and associated companies in
Berlin Ibadan

Oxford is a trade mark of Oxford University Press

Not for sale in the USA

ISBN 0 19 148176 9

First published 1994

10 9 8 7 6 5 4 3 2 1

Music and text origination by
Barnes Music Engraving Ltd., East Sussex
and Oxuniprint

Printed in Great Britain by
Richard Clay Ltd., Bungay, Suffolk

A Words Edition is also available

Contents

Foreword

Aware of growing interest in examples of new hymnody, and following the Special Assembly held the previous year in Coleraine (when music in the contemporary idiom had received particular emphasis), the General Assembly of 1991 appointed a committee to prepare a supplement to the standard hymnaries of the Presbyterian Church in Ireland.

Consultation with Presbyteries, with other organizations, and with interested individuals served both to identify what was in common use and to highlight whole areas of resource which had been hitherto untapped. A period of intensive research produced a wealth of material, and a process of sifting and culling from this has resulted in the present selection. It is comprehensive but by no means exhaustive, and reflects the committee's remit to provide a supplement rather than another, alternative, hymn-book. The final selection duly received the approval of the Assembly in 1992.

On the one hand, this supplement is designed to facilitate the task of those who are already familiar with much of the material it contains, and to provide a means of extending their existing repertoire. On the other, we hope to encourage those ministers and congregations, choirs, and leaders who perhaps have been reluctant to come to terms with current trends in music to experiment in this field.

Much that has been traditional will continue to be of value to many who worship in our churches. But the psalmist's call to 'Sing a new song to the Lord' is as much to our own age as to his, and encourages the use of words and music which give contemporary expression to a contemporary faith. The compilers of this book, bringing to their task a variety of interests and experience, have sought to be true to that aim, while maintaining the high standards in musical, poetical, and theological language which alone are worthy of the God they address, and which enable those who would sing from the heart to sing also with understanding.

As it reflects the needs and responds to the desires of many in the Church today, this supplement is offered, confidently yet humbly, as an aid to worship, with the prayer that the work of the committee, the material in the book itself, and the praises of all who avail of it may indeed combine to bring glory to God.

JOHN F. MURDOCH
Convener, Public Worship Committee
Co-Convener, Hymnal Supplement Committee

Preface

The title chosen for this supplementary hymnal—*Glory to God*—expresses the central theme and purpose of worship within the Reformed tradition, and the concern of the committee in the compilation of the book. This theme is carried through the four sections into which we have divided the material.

The first section, 'Glory to God', contains general ascriptions of praise to God, Father, Son, and Holy Spirit, and the material in it is particularly suited to the opening of worship or times when we wish to affirm our faith. 'Glory to God in Personal Experience' comes next, and contains more personal expressions of desire after and thanksgiving for the presence of God in our lives. 'Glory to God in the Church' deals with the corporate issues of our faith, and includes hymns on such specific matters as the scriptures and the sacraments. Finally, 'Glory to God in the World' rouses us to our responsibilities as Christians towards creation and mission.

In an attempt to make the book easy to use, material is loosely alphabetically arranged within each section, where the layout of the items permits. In addition, indexing has been provided at the back of the book, including an extensive index of themes.

The committee has tried to ensure that the tunes selected are appropriate to the words to which they are set, and we hope that congregations will make the effort to become familiar with music that is new to them. On occasions, however, we have provided references to alternative tunes which may be more familiar and are to be found within the present book or in the *Revised Church Hymnary* and the *Church Hymnary: Third Edition*, the two hymnals currently in use in our denomination.

The hymns included in the book reflect the wide variety of styles to be found in contemporary praise. There are hymns to existing tunes and to new tunes; new psalm settings; songs in a contemporary style from composers such as Graham Kendrick; songs set to traditional folk tunes, or to new tunes written in that idiom from such sources as the Iona Community; songs from the world Church—from places as far apart as South Africa and Nicaragua; songs suited to children; and a few older hymns omitted from *Revised Church Hymnary* or *Church Hymnary: Third Edition*.

Obviously, difficult choices had to be made. Early in its work the committee determined on some simple guidelines regarding the type of material to be included. For example, songs with only one verse are easily displayed on an overhead projector or included in a printed order of service, and so were excluded from consideration. Hymns available in *Revised Church Hymnary* or *Church Hymnary: Third Edition* were also excluded, with three well-known exceptions. Where appropriate, revisions of older hymns in more contemporary language have been selected in preference to the originals, and inclusive language has been adopted where possible.

This hymn-book is designed to augment the congregational praise on a Sunday, and not to become the book used only at the mid-week meeting, PWA, or Youth Fellowship. As a result, the hymns selected are intended for *all* to sing, although many would lend themselves to four-part singing as an occasional anthem by the choir. Instrumental descants and guitar chords have been provided where appropriate, and most of the hymns would benefit from instrumental accompaniment in addition to or instead of the traditional organ. Some of the pieces, especially those from non-European sources, are most suited to unaccompanied singing and will enable congregations to explore the richness of the human voice on its own in the praise of God.

This book is the fruit of a great deal of hard work. The committee would like to thank all those who have helped us in bringing it to fruition, and in particular Mrs Helen Killick, our part-time administrative officer, Mr Oswald McAuley, secretary to the committee, and Mr Richard McChesney, who handled publicity. We would also wish to express our gratitude to the Oxford University Press and its representatives, for their helpfulness and expertise.

The committee hopes that congregations will experiment with the various styles and musical moods offered by this book. It is designed to have a life-span of seven to ten years, during which time its purpose is to foster a spirit of openness towards new songs and modern forms of expressing our love for God. Used sensitively beside *Revised Church Hymnary* or *Church Hymnary: Third Edition* we believe it will provide our congregations with the best of old and new in corporate praise. We hope that it will greatly enhance our worship, in the spirit of its title.

JOHN R. DICKINSON
Co-Convener, Hymnal Supplement Committee

Addresses of main copyright holders

The Presbyterian Church in Ireland and Oxford University Press are grateful to those who have given permission for copyright material to be included. Every effort has been made to trace copyright owners, and apologies are extended to anyone whose rights have inadvertently not been acknowledged. Any omissions or inaccuracies of copyright detail will be corrected in subsequent printings if valid claims have been received by the publisher.

Copyright details will be found at the foot of each item in the book. The addresses of the main copyright holders are listed below, and others appear at the foot of the relevant items in the book. For any information not included, or for permission to use material controlled by Oxford University Press, please write to the Hymn Copyright Manager, Oxford University Press, 3 Park Road, London NW1 6XN, enclosing a reply-paid envelope.

Timothy Dudley-Smith
9 Ashlands
Ford
Salisbury
Wiltshire SP4 6DY

Hope Publishing Company
Carol Stream
IL 60188
USA

Jubilate Hymns Ltd.
61 Chessel Avenue
Southampton SO2 4DY

Kingsway's Thankyou Music Ltd.
PO Box 75
Eastbourne
East Sussex BN23 6NW

Little Misty Music
PO Box 8
Perth PH2 7EX
Scotland

Make Way Music
PO Box 263
Croydon CR9 5AP

The Scripture Union
130 City Road
London EC1V 2NJ

Sovereign Lifestyle Music
PO Box 356
Leighton Buzzard
Bedfordshire LU7 8WP

Stainer & Bell Ltd.
PO Box 110
Victoria House
23 Gruneisen Road
London N3 1DZ

Josef Weinberger Ltd.
12–14 Mortimer Street
London W1N 7RD

Wild Goose Publications
Pearce Institute
Govan
Glasgow G51 3UT
Scotland

1 All heaven declares

All heaven declares

Noel and Tricia Richards
arr. Helen Killick (b. 1965)

1. All heav'n de - clares____ the glo - ry of the
all heav'n de - clares

ri - sen Lord. Who can com - pare____
who can com -

_ with the beau-ty of the Lord? For-ev - er he will
- pare _

All heaven declares
the glory of the risen Lord.
Who can compare
with the beauty of the Lord?
Forever he will be
the Lamb upon the throne.
I gladly bow the knee
and worship him alone.

2 I will proclaim
the glory of the risen Lord
who once was slain
to reconcile us to God.
Forever you will be
the Lamb upon the throne.
I gladly bow the knee
and worship you alone.

Noel and Tricia Richards

3

2 Be still, for the presence of the Lord

Be still

Dave Evans (b. 1957)
arr. Helen Killick (b. 1965)

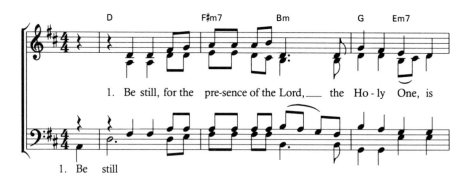

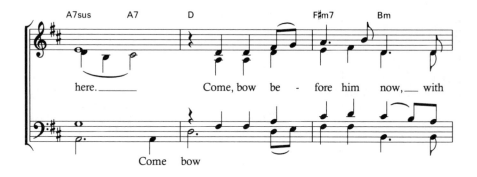

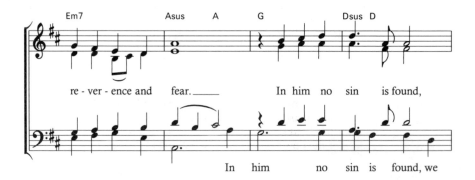

GLORY TO GOD

Be still, for the presence of the Lord, the Holy One, is here.
Come, bow before him now, with reverence and fear.
In him no sin is found, we stand on holy ground.
Be still, for the presence of the Lord, the Holy One, is here.

2 Be still, for the glory of the Lord is shining all around;
   he burns with holy fire, with splendour he is crowned.
   How awesome is the sight, our radiant King of light!
   Be still, for the glory of the Lord is shining all around.

3 Be still, for the power of the Lord is moving in this place,
   he comes to cleanse and heal, to minister his grace.
   No work too hard for him, in faith receive from him;
   be still, for the power of the Lord is moving in this place.

Dave Evans (b. 1957)

5

3 I am for you

Incarnation   64 64 66 64   *John Bell (b. 1949)*

Before the world began,
one Word was there;
grounded in God he was,
rooted in care;
by him all things were made,
in him was love displayed,
through him God spoke, and said,
'I am for you.'

2   Life found in him its source,
death found its end;
light found in him its course,
darkness its friend.
For neither death nor doubt
nor darkness can put out
the glow of God, the shout,
'I am for you.'

3   The Word was in the world
which from him came;
unrecognized he was,
unknown by name;
one with all humankind,
with the unloved aligned,
convincing sight and mind,
'I am for you.'

4   All who received the Word
by God were blessed;
sisters and brothers they
of earth's fond guest.
So did the Word of grace
proclaim in time and space
and with a human face,
'I am for you.'

John Bell (b. 1949) and Graham Maule (b. 1958)
from John 1: 1–13

4 Bring to the Lord a glad new song

Jerusalem DLM

Charles H. H. Parry (1848–1918)

1. Bring to the Lord a glad new song, child-ren of grace ex - tol your king: your love and praise to God be -

crea-ture praise the Lord!

2. Sing praise with - in   these hal - lowed walls,   wor-ship be -

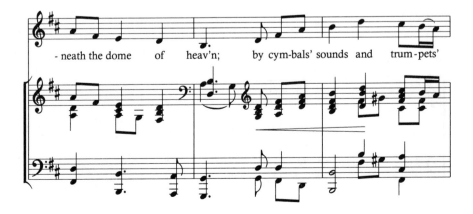

- neath the dome   of   heav'n;   by cym-bals' sounds and   trum-pets'

calls   let prai-ses   fit   for God   be   given: with strings and

brass   and wind re - joice— then, join our   song   in   full ac -

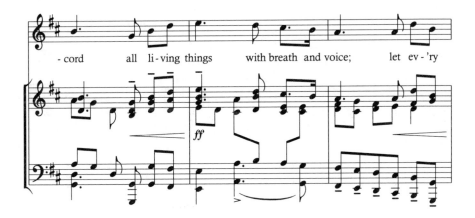

- cord   all li - ving things   with breath and voice;   let ev - 'ry

GLORY TO GOD

crea-ture praise the Lord!

Bring to the Lord a glad new song,
children of grace extol your king:
your love and praise to God belong—
to instruments of music, sing!
Let those be warned who spurn God's name,
let rulers all obey God's word,
for justice shall bring tyrants shame—
let every creature praise the Lord!

2   Sing praise within these hallowed walls,
worship beneath the dome of heaven;
by cymbals' sounds and trumpets' calls
let praises fit for God be given:
with strings and brass and wind rejoice—
then, join our song in full accord
all living things with breath and voice;
let every creature praise the Lord!

Michael Perry (b. 1942)
from Psalms 149 and 150

12

5 He was pierced for our transgressions

Like a lamb

Words and music by Maggi Dawn (b. 1959)
Words from Isaiah 53: 5–8

1. He was pierced for___ our trans - gres - sions,___
(2.) led like a lamb to the slaugh-ter,___

and bruised for___ our in - i - qui -
al - though he was in - no - cent of

- ties;
crime;

and to bring us___
and cut off from the

peace he was pun-ished,___
land of the li - ving,___

and by his___
he paid for the

13

GLORY TO GOD

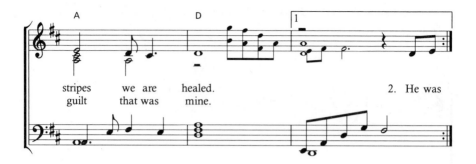

stripes   we are   healed.
guilt   that was   mine.

2. He was

DESCANT (*on repeat of refrain*)

lamb, _____ like a lamb, _

REFRAIN

We like sheep have gone a -

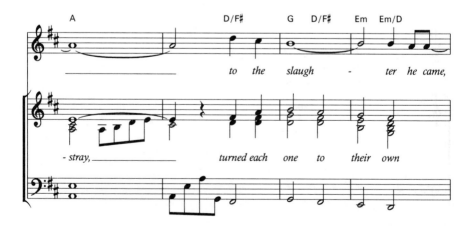

to the slaugh - ter he came,

- stray, _____ turned each one to their own

GLORY TO GOD

and the Lord_____ laid on
way,_____ and the Lord has laid on

him_____ the in - i - qui - ty of us
him_____ the in - i - qui - ty of us

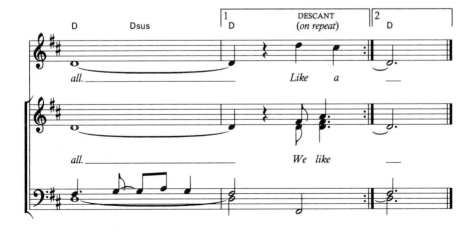

all._____ Like a ___
all._____ We like ___

6 Christ is alive

Old Clarendonian 88 88 (LM) *Olwen Wonnacott (b. 1930)*

Alternative tune: TRURO, *Church Hymnary: Third Edition* no. 446, *Revised Church Hymnary* no. 369

Christ is alive! Let Christians sing;
the cross stands empty to the sky;
let streets and homes with praises ring;
love drowned in death shall never die.

2 Christ is alive! No longer bound
to distant years in Palestine;
but saving, healing, here and now,
and touching every place and time.

3 Not throned afar, remotely high,
untouched, unmoved by human pains,
but daily, in the midst of life,
our Saviour in the Godhead reigns.

4 In every insult, rift and war,
where colour, scorn or wealth divide,
he suffers still, yet loves the more,
and lives where even hope has died.

5 Christ is alive, and comes to bring
new life to this and every age,
till earth and all creation ring
with joy, with justice, love, and praise.

Brian Wren (b. 1936)

7 Christ is the world's Light

Christe Sanctorum   10 11 11 6

Melody from Paris Antiphoner, 1681
arr. David Iliff (b. 1939)

Christ is the world's Light, he and none other;
born in our darkness, he became our brother.
If we have seen him, we have seen the Father:
Glory to God on high.

2 Christ is the world's Peace, he and none other;
no man can serve him and despise his brother.
Who else unites us, one in God the Father?
Glory to God on high.

3 Christ is the world's Life, he and none other;
sold once for silver, murdered here, our brother—
he, who redeems us, reigns with God the Father:
Glory to God on high.

4 Give God the glory, God and none other;
give God the glory, Spirit, Son and Father;
give God the glory, God in Man my brother:
Glory to God on high.

Fred Pratt Green (b. 1903)

8 Christer triumphant

FIRST TUNE

Christ triumphant   88 85 with refrain

Michael Baughen (b. 1930)
arr. Noël Tredinnick (b. 1949)

1. Christ tri - umph - ant, e - ver reign - ing, Sa - viour, Mas - ter, King!_____ Lord of heav'n, our lives sus - tain - ing, hear us as we sing:_____

REFRAIN

Yours the glo - ry and the crown,_____ the high

re - nown,_____ the e - ter - nal name._____

Christ triumphant, ever reigning,
Saviour, Master, King!
Lord of heaven, our lives sustaining,
hear us as we sing:

Yours the glory and the crown,
the high renown, the eternal name!

2 Word incarnate, truth revealing,
Son of Man on earth!
Power and majesty concealing
by your humble birth:

3 Suffering servant, scorned, ill-treated,
victim crucified!
Death is through the cross defeated,
sinners justified:

4 Priestly King, enthroned for ever
high in heaven above!
Sin and death and hell shall never
stifle hymns of love:

5 So, our hearts and voices raising
through the ages long,
ceaselessly upon you gazing,
this shall be our song:

Michael Saward (b. 1932)

(8) Christ triumphant

SECOND TUNE

Guiting Power   85 85 with refrain   *John Barnard (b. 1948)*

crown, the high re - nown,_____ the e - ter - nal name!

and the crown, the high re - nown, th' e - ter - nal name!

Christ triumphant, ever reigning,
Saviour, Master, King!
Lord of heaven, our lives sustaining,
hear us as we sing:

Yours the glory and the crown,
the high renown, the eternal name!

2 Word incarnate, truth revealing,
Son of Man on earth!
Power and majesty concealing
by your humble birth:

3 Suffering servant, scorned, ill-treated,
victim crucified!
Death is through the cross defeated,
sinners justified:

4 Priestly King, enthroned for ever
high in heaven above!
Sin and death and hell shall never
stifle hymns of love:

5 So, our hearts and voices raising
through the ages long,
ceaselessly upon you gazing,
this shall be our song:

Michael Saward (b. 1932)

9 God has spoken—by his prophets

Ebenezer 87 87 D

Thomas Williams (1869–1944)

God has spoken—by his prophets,
spoken his unchanging word;
each from age to age proclaiming
God the one, the righteous Lord;
in the world's despair and turmoil
one firm anchor still holds fast:
God is King, his throne eternal,
God the first and God the last.

2   God has spoken—by Christ Jesus,
Christ, the everlasting Son;
brightness of the Father's glory,
with the Father ever one:
spoken by the Word incarnate,
Life, before all time began,
light of light, to earth descending,
God, revealed as Son of Man.

3   God is speaking—by his Spirit
speaking to our hearts again;
in the age-long word expounding
God's own message, now as then.
Through the rise and fall of nations
one sure faith is standing fast:
God abides, his word unchanging,
God the first and God the last.

George Wallace Briggs (1875–1959)

10 God is love

Abbot's Leigh   87 87 D

Cyril Taylor (1907–91)

Alternative tune: BLAENWERN, *Church Hymnary: Third Edition* no. 473

God is love: let heaven adore him;
God is love: let earth rejoice;
let creation sing before him,
and exalt him with one voice.
He who laid the earth's foundation,
he who spread the heavens above,
he who breathes through all creation,
he is love, eternal love.

2 God is love, and is enfolding
all the world in one embrace;
his unfailing grasp is holding
every child of every race;
and when human hearts are breaking
under sorrow's iron rod,
that same sorrow, that same aching
wrings with pain the heart of God.

3 God is love: and though with blindness
sin afflicts and clouds the will,
God's eternal loving-kindness
holds us fast and guides us still.
Sin and death and hell shall never
o'er us final triumph gain;
God is love, so Love for ever
o'er the universe must reign.

Timothy Rees (1874–1939)

11 God is our strength and refuge

Dambusters' March   77 75 77 11

Eric Coates (1886–1958)
arr. Robin Sheldon (b. 1932)

God is our strength and refuge,
our present help in trouble;
and we therefore will not fear,
though the earth should change!
Though mountains shake and tremble,
though swirling floods are raging,
God the Lord of hosts is with us evermore!

2 There is a flowing river,
within God's holy city;
God is in the midst of her—
she shall not be moved!
God's help is swiftly given,
thrones vanish at his presence—
God the Lord of hosts is with us evermore!

3 Come, see the works of our maker,
learn of his deeds all-powerful;
wars will cease across the world
when he shatters the spear!
Be still and know your creator,
uplift him in the nations—
God the Lord of hosts is with us evermore!

Richard Bewes (b. 1934)
from Psalm 46

12 Great is thy faithfulness

Faithfulness 11 10 11 10 with refrain   *William Runyan (1870–1957)*

Great is thy faith-ful-ness! Great is thy faith-ful-ness! Morn-ing by

morn - ing new mer - cies I see; all I have need - ed thy

hand hath pro - vid - ed— great is thy faith - ful-ness, Lord, un - to me!

Great is thy faithfulness, O God my Father,
there is no shadow of turning with thee;
thou changest not, thy compassions they fail not,
as thou hast been thou for ever wilt be.

Great is thy faithfulness!
Great is thy faithfulness!
Morning by morning new mercies I see;
all I have needed thy hand hath provided—
great is thy faithfulness, Lord, unto me!

2 Summer and winter, and spring-time and harvest,
sun, moon and stars in their courses above,
join with all nature in manifold witness
to thy great faithfulness, mercy and love.

3 Pardon for sin and a peace that endureth,
thine own dear presence to cheer and to guide;
strength for today and bright hope for tomorrow,
blessings all mine, with ten thousand beside!

Thomas Chisholm (1866–1960)

13 He gave his life in selfless love

Selfless love   86 86 D (DCM)   *Andrew Maries (b. 1949)*

He gave his life in selfless love,
for sinners once he came;
he had no stain of sin himself
but bore our guilt and shame:
he took the cup of pain and death,
his blood was freely shed;
we see his body on the cross,
we share the living bread.

2   He did not come to call the good
but sinners to repent;
it was the lame, the deaf, the blind
for whom his life was spent:
to heal the sick, to find the lost—
it was for such he came,
and round his table all may come
to praise his holy name.

3   They heard him call his Father's name—
then, 'Finished!' was his cry;
like them we have forsaken him
and left him there to die:
the sins that crucified him then
are sins his blood has cured;
the love that bound him to a cross
our freedom has ensured.

4   His body broken once for us
is glorious now above;
the cup of blessing we receive,
a sharing of his love:
as in his presence we partake,
his dying we proclaim
until the hour of majesty
when Jesus comes again.

Christopher Porteous (b. 1935)

14 How good it is to sing

How good it is

Words and music by Ian White (b. 1956)
Words from Psalm 147: 1–6
Music arr. Helen Killick (b. 1965)

Lively
Unison

How good it is to sing praise to our God,

the right and plea-sant thing to praise his name.

The Lord is build-ing up Je - ru - sa - lem,

he ga-thers all the lost of Is - ra - el.

He is heal-ing the bro-ken - heart-ed, he is bind-ing all their wounds,

he de - ter-mines the stars in the hea - vens and he calls them each by name.

Great is the Lord in pow'r, all things he knows,

he casts the wick-ed down, but lifts the low.

35

15 Jesus is Lord

Jesus is Lord 11 12 11 12 with refrain

Words and music by
David Mansell (b. 1936)

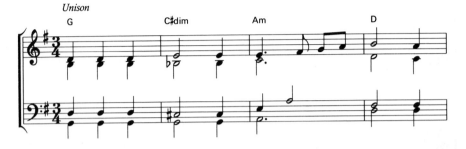

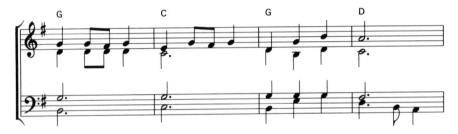

Jesus is Lord! Creation's voice proclaims it,
for by his power each tree and flower was planned and made.
Jesus is Lord! The universe declares it—
sun, moon and stars in heaven cry: 'Jesus is Lord!'

Jesus is Lord, Jesus is Lord!
Praise him with alleluias,
for Jesus is Lord!

2 Jesus is Lord! Yet from his throne eternal
in flesh he came to die in pain on Calvary's tree.
Jesus is Lord! From him all life proceeding—
yet gave his life a ransom thus setting us free.

3 Jesus is Lord! O'er sin the mighty conqueror;
from death he rose, and all his foes shall own his name.
Jesus is Lord! God sent his Holy Spirit
to show by works of power that Jesus is Lord!

David Mansell (b. 1936)

37

16 Jesus the Lord said, 'I am the bread'

Yisu ne kaha

Urdu traditional melody
arr. Helen Killick (b. 1965)

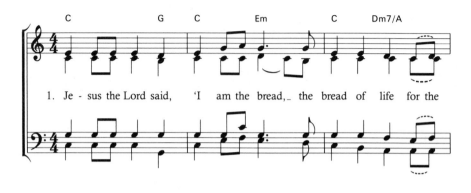

1. Je - sus the Lord said, 'I am the bread,_ the bread of life for the

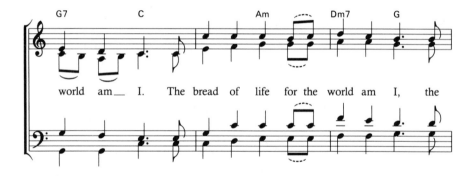

world am_ I. The bread of life for the world am I, the

bread of_ life for the world am_ I.'___ Je - sus the Lord said,

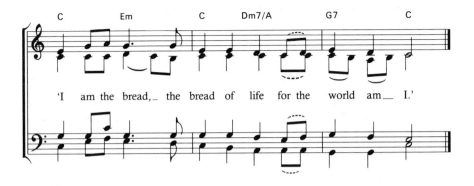

'I am the bread,_ the bread of life for the world am_ I.'

Jesus the Lord said, 'I am the bread,
the bread of life for the world am I.
The bread of life for the world am I,
the bread of life for the world am I.'
Jesus the Lord said, 'I am the bread,
the bread of life for the world am I.'

2   Jesus the Lord said, 'I am the vine,
the true and fruitful vine am I.'

3   Jesus the Lord said, 'I am the way,
the true and living way am I.'

4   Jesus the Lord said, 'I am the light,
the one true light of the world am I.'

5   Jesus the Lord said, 'I am the life,

the resurrection and the life am I.'

vv. 1, 3–5: Anon.,
tr. from Urdu C. D. Monahan (1906–57)
v. 2: Compilers of 'Rejoice and Sing', 1991

17 Jesus! the name high over all

Lydia   86 86 (CM) extended

Thomas Phillips (1735–1807)

Jesus! the name high over all
in hell or earth or sky;
angels again before it fall
and devils fear and fly,
and devils fear and fly.

2   Jesus! the name to sinners dear,
the name to sinners given;
it scatters all their guilty fear,
it turns their hell to heaven,
it turns their hell to heaven.

3   Jesus the prisoner's fetters breaks
and bruises Satan's head;
power into strengthless souls he speaks
and life into the dead,
and life into the dead.

4   O that the world might taste and see
the riches of his grace!
The arms of love that welcome me
would all mankind embrace,
would all mankind embrace.

5   His righteousness alone I show,
his saving grace proclaim;
this is my work on earth below,
to cry, 'Behold the Lamb!'
to cry, 'Behold the Lamb!'

6   Happy if with my final breath
I may but gasp his name,
preach him to all, and cry in death,
'Christ Jesus is the Lamb!'
'Christ Jesus is the Lamb!'

Charles Wesley (1707–88)

18 Like a mighty river flowing

Old Yeavering 888 7 *Noël Tredinnick (b. 1949)*

Alternative tune: QUEM PASTORES LAUDAVERE, *Church Hymnary: Third Edition* no. 111, *Revised Church Hymnary* no. 349

Like a mighty river flowing,
like a flower in beauty growing,
far beyond all human knowing
is the perfect peace of God.

2 Like the hills serene and even,
like the coursing clouds of heaven,
like the heart that's been forgiven
is the perfect peace of God.

3 Like the summer breezes playing,
like the tall trees softly swaying,
like the lips of silent praying
is the perfect peace of God.

4 Like the morning sun ascended,
like the scents of evening blended,
like a friendship never ended
is the perfect peace of God.

5 Like the azure ocean swelling,
like the jewel all-excelling,
far beyond our human telling
is the perfect peace of God.

Michael Perry (b. 1942)

19 Meekness and majesty

Meekness and majesty

Words and music by
Graham Kendrick (b. 1950)

1. Meek-ness and ma-jes-ty, man-hood and de-i-ty,
2. Fa-ther's pure ra-di-ance, per-fect in in-no-cence,
3. Wis-dom un-search-a-ble, God the in-vi-si-ble;

in per-fect har-mo-ny, the man who is God.
yet learns o-be-di-ence to death on a cross.
love in-de-struc-ti-ble in frail-ty ap-pears.

Lord of e-ter-ni-ty dwells in hu-ma-ni-ty,
Suf-fering to give us life, con-quering through sa-cri-fice;
Lord of in-fi-ni-ty stoop-ing so ten-der-ly

GLORY TO GOD

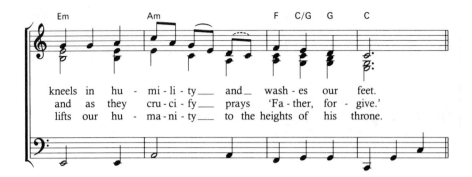

kneels in hu - mi - li - ty___ and___ wash - es our feet.
and as they cru - ci - fy___ prays 'Fa - ther, for - give.'
lifts our hu - ma - ni - ty___ to the heights of his throne.

REFRAIN

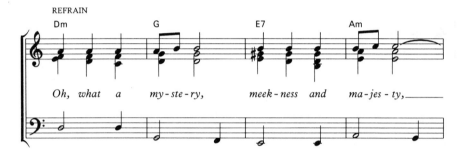

Oh, what a my - ste - ry, meek - ness and ma - jes - ty,___

___ bow down and wor - ship,___

___ for this is your God,___

44

GLORY TO GOD

this   is   your

1, 2

God.

3

God,

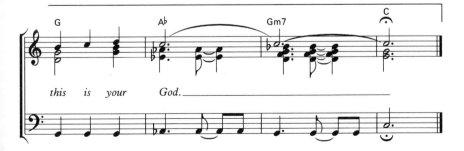

this   is   your   God.

20 Lord, you were rich beyond all splendour

Bergers (Quelle est cette odeur)   98 98 98

French traditional melody
arr. Martin Shaw (1875–1958)

Lord, you were rich beyond all splendour,
yet, for love's sake, became so poor;
leaving your throne in glad surrender,
sapphire-paved courts for stable floor:
Lord, you were rich beyond all splendour,
yet, for love's sake, became so poor.

2　You are our God beyond all praising,
yet, for love's sake, became a man;
stooping so low, but sinners raising
heavenwards, by your eternal plan:
you are our God, beyond all praising,
yet, for love's sake, became a man.

3　Lord, you are love beyond all telling,
Saviour and King, we worship you;
Emmanuel, within us dwelling,
make us and keep us pure and true:
Lord, you are love beyond all telling,
Saviour and King, we worship you.

F. Houghton (1894–1972)

21   Name of all majesty

Majestas   66 55 66 64

Michael Baughen (b. 1930)
arr. Noël Tredinnick (b. 1949)

Name of all majesty,
fathomless mystery,
king of the ages
by angels adored;
power and authority,
splendour and dignity,
bow to his mastery—
Jesus is Lord!

2 Child of our destiny,
God from eternity,
love of the Father
on sinners outpoured;
see now what God has done
sending his only son,
Christ the beloved one—
Jesus is Lord!

3 Saviour of Calvary,
costliest victory,
darkness defeated
and Eden restored;
born as a man to die
nailed to a cross on high,
cold in the grave to lie—
Jesus is Lord!

4 Source of all sovereignty,
light, immortality,
life everlasting
and heaven assured;
so with the ransomed, we
praise him eternally,
Christ in his majesty—
Jesus is Lord!

Timothy Dudley-Smith (b. 1926)

22 O God beyond all praising

Thaxted 13 13 13 13 13 13

Gustav Holst (1874–1934)

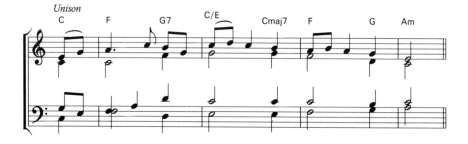

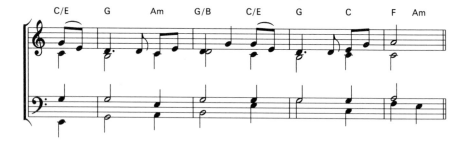

O God beyond all praising,
we worship you today
and sing the love amazing
that songs cannot repay;
for we can only wonder
at every gift you send,
at blessings without number
and mercies without end:
we lift our hearts before you
and wait upon your word,
we honour and adore you,
our great and mighty Lord.

2 Then hear, O gracious Saviour,
accept the love we bring,
that we who know your favour
may serve you as our King;
and whether our tomorrows
be filled with good or ill,
we'll triumph through our sorrows
and rise to bless you still:
to marvel at your beauty
and glory in your ways,
and make a joyful duty
our sacrifice of praise!

Michael Perry (b. 1942)

23 How great thou art!

How great thou art   11 10 11 10 with refrain

Swedish traditional melody
arr. Stuart Hine (1899–1989)

Then sings my soul, my Sa-viour God, to thee, How great thou

GLORY TO GOD

O Lord my God, when I in awesome wonder
consider all the works thy hand hath made,
I see the stars, I hear the mighty thunder,
thy power throughout the universe displayed;

Then sings my soul, my Saviour God, to thee,
How great thou art! How great thou art!
Then sings my soul, my Saviour God, to thee,
How great thou art! How great thou art!

2   When through the woods and forest glades I wander
and hear the birds sing sweetly in the trees;
when I look down from lofty mountain grandeur,
and hear the brook, and feel the gentle breeze;

3   And when I think that God his son not sparing,
sent him to die—I scarce can take it in,
that on the cross my burden gladly bearing,
he bled and died to take away my sin:

4   When Christ shall come with shout of acclamation
and take me home—what joy shall fill my heart!
then shall I bow in humble adoration
and there proclaim, my God, how great thou art!

Russian hymn
tr. Stuart Hine (1899–1989)

24 Praise be to Christ

Ye banks and braes   88 88 D (DLM)

Scottish traditional melody
arr. Norman Warren (b. 1934)

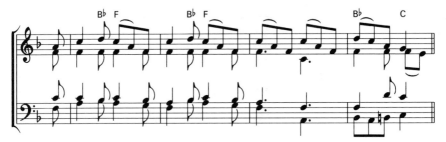

An alternative arrangement of this tune (in G) may be found at no. 103.

Praise be to Christ in whom we see
the image of the Father shown,
the first-born Son revealed and known,
the truth and grace of deity;
through whom creation came to birth,
whose fingers set the stars in place,
the unseen powers, and this small earth,
the furthest bounds of time and space.

2　Praise be to him whose sovereign sway
and will upholds creation's plan;
who is, before all worlds began
and when our world has passed away:
Lord of the Church, its life and head,
redemption's price and source and theme,
alive, the first-born from the dead,
to reign as all-in-all supreme.

3　Praise be to him who, Lord most high,
the fullness of the Godhead shares;
and yet our human nature bears,
who came as man to bleed and die:
and from his cross there flows our peace
who chose for us the path he trod,
that so might sins and sorrows cease
and all be reconciled to God.

Timothy Dudley-Smith (b. 1926)
from Colossians 1: 15–20

25 Sing a new song

Onslow Square   7 7 11 8

David Wilson (b. 1940)

1. Sing a new song to the Lord, he to whom won-ders be-

-long;_____ re - joice_____ in his tri - umph___ and

tell_____ of his pow'r—_____ O sing_____ to the

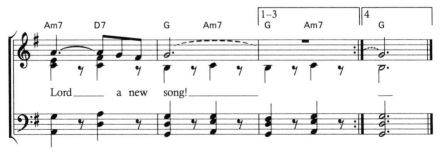

Lord_____ a new song!_____

Words © T. Dudley-Smith. Music © D. Wilson/Jubilate Hymns.

Sing a new song to the Lord,
he to whom wonders belong;
rejoice in his triumph and tell of his power—
O sing to the Lord a new song!

2 Now to the ends of the earth
see his salvation is shown;
and still he remembers his mercy and truth,
unchanging in love to his own.

3 Sing a new song and rejoice,
publish his praises abroad;
let voices in chorus, with trumpet and horn,
resound for the joy of the Lord!

4 Join with the hills and the sea
thunders of praise to prolong:
in judgement and justice he comes to the earth—
O sing to the Lord a new song!

Timothy Dudley-Smith (b. 1926)
from Psalm 98

26 Sing of the Lord's goodness

Sing of the Lord's goodness

Words and music by Ernest Sands
Descant by Christopher Walker
arr. Paul Inwood

1. Sing of the Lord's good-ness, Fa-ther of all wis-dom, come to him and bless his name._____ Mer-cy he has shown us, his love is for e-ver,
2. Po-wer he has wield-ed, hon-our is his gar-ment, ri-sen from the snares of death._____ His word he has spo-ken, one bread he has bro-ken,
3. Cour-age in our dark-ness, com-fort in our sor-row—Spi-rit of our God most high!_____ Sol-ace for the wea-ry, par-don for the sin-ner,
4. Praise him with your sing-ing, praise him with the trum-pet, praise God with the lute and harp!_____ Praise him with the cym-bals, praise him with your dan-cing,

GLORY TO GOD

Am7   **Bm7**   **Em**   **REFRAIN**   **Am7**   **D**

DESCANT
You peo - ple come _____

faith - ful to the end of days. _____
new life he now gives to all. _____
splen-dour of the liv - ing God! _____
praise God till the end of days. _____

Come then all you na-tions,

Gmaj7   **Am**   **B7**

sing _____ praise, sing praise to

sing of your Lord's good - ness, me - lo - dies of praise and

Em   **Am7**   **D**

God. Come and ring out the Lord's glo - ry,

thanks to God; ring out the Lord's glo - ry,

GLORY TO GOD

praise him with your mu - sic, wor - ship him and bless his

praise him with your mu - sic, wor - ship him and bless his

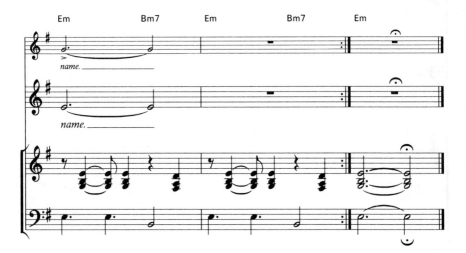

name. name.

Alternative accompaniment rhythm:

etc.

27 This earth belongs to God

Prince of Denmark's March

Jeremiah Clarke (c.1674–1707)
arr. Helen Killick (b. 1965)

Words © C. Idle/Jubilate Hymns. Arrangement: Presbyterian Church in Ireland/Oxford University Press.

On-ly the one whose heart is pure, whose hands and lips   are clean.

This earth belongs to God,
the world, its wealth and all its people;
he formed the waters wide
and fashioned every sea and shore.

(*Group A*)   Who may go up the hill of the Lord
and stand in the place of holiness?

(*Group B*)   Only the one whose heart is pure,
whose hands and lips are clean.

2   Lift high your heads, you gates,
rise up, you everlasting doors,
as here now the King of glory
enters into full command.

(*Group A*)   Who is the King, this King of glory,
where is the throne he comes to claim?

(*Group B*)   Christ is the King, the Lord of glory,
fresh from his victory.

3   Lift high your heads, you gates,
and fling wide open the ancient doors,
for here comes the King of glory
taking universal power.

(*Group A*)   Who is the King, this King of glory,
what is the power by which he reigns?

(*Group B*)   Christ is the King, his cross his glory,
and by love he rules.

4   All glory be to God
the Father, Son and Holy Spirit;
from ages past it was,
is now, and ever more shall be.

Christopher Idle (b. 1938)
from Psalm 24

The second half of each verse is best sung by two groups, A and B.   *(instrumental parts overleaf)*

TUNE (for B♭ instruments)

DESCANT (for B♭ instruments)
(for bars 1–8 Da Capo only)

28 Sing to God

Ode to Joy   87 87 D   *Ludwig van Beethoven (1770–1827)*

Words © M. Baughen/Jubilate Hymns.

Sing to God new songs of worship—
all his deeds are marvellous;
he has brought salvation to us
with his hand and holy arm:
he has shown to all the nations
righteousness and saving power;
he recalled his truth and mercy
to his people Israel.

2   Sing to God new songs of worship—
earth has seen his victory;
let the lands of earth be joyful
praising him with thankfulness:
sound upon the harp with praises,
play to him with melody;
let the trumpets sound his triumph,
show your joy to God the King!

3   Sing to God new songs of worship—
let the sea now make a noise;
all on earth and in the waters
sound your praises to the Lord:
let the hills rejoice together,
let the rivers clap their hands,
for with righteousness and justice
he will come to judge the earth.

Michael Baughen (b. 1930)
from Psalm 98

29 Tell out, my soul

Woodlands   10 10 10 10   *Walter Greatorex (1877–1949)*

Alternative tune: YANWORTH, no. 80

Words © T. Dudley-Smith. Music © Oxford University Press.

Tell out, my soul, the greatness of the Lord:
unnumbered blessings, give my spirit voice;
tender to me the promise of his word;
in God my Saviour shall my heart rejoice.

2   Tell out, my soul, the greatness of his name:
make known his might, the deeds his arm has done;
his mercy sure, from age to age the same;
his holy name, the Lord, the Mighty One.

3   Tell out, my soul, the greatness of his might:
powers and dominions lay their glory by;
proud hearts and stubborn wills are put to flight,
the hungry fed, the humble lifted high.

4   Tell out, my soul, the glories of his word:
firm is his promise, and his mercy sure.
Tell out, my soul, the greatness of the Lord
to children's children and for evermore.

Timothy Dudley-Smith (b. 1926)
from the Magnificat (Luke 1: 46–55)

30 There is a Redeemer

There is a Redeemer

Melody Green
arr. Norman Warren (b. 1934)

1. There is a Re - deem - er, Je - sus, God's own Son,
2. Je - sus, my Re - deem - er, name a - bove all names,
3. When I stand in glo - ry, I will see his face, and

precious Lamb of God, Mes - si - ah, Ho - ly One.
precious Lamb of God, Mes - si - ah, O for sin - ners slain.
there I'll serve my King for e - ver in that ho - ly place.

REFRAIN

Thank you, O my Fa - ther, for gi - ving us your Son, and

lea - ving your Spi - rit till the work on— earth is done.——

There is a Redeemer,
Jesus, God's own Son,
precious Lamb of God, Messiah,
Holy One.

Thank you, O my Father,
for giving us your Son,
and leaving your Spirit
till the work on earth is done.

2 Jesus, my Redeemer,
name above all names,
precious Lamb of God, Messiah,
O for sinners slain.

3 When I stand in glory,
I will see his face,
and there I'll serve my King for ever
in that holy place.

Melody Green

31 Thine be the glory

Maccabaeus   10 11 11 11 and refrain   *Georg Frideric Handel (1685–1759)*

REFRAIN

Thine be the glo - ry,

ri - sen, con-qu'ring Son,   end-less is the   vic - t'ry   thou o'er death hast won.

Thine be the glory, risen, conquering Son,
endless is the victory thou o'er death hast won;
angels in bright raiment rolled the stone away,
kept the folded grave-clothes, where thy body lay.

Thine be the glory, risen, conquering Son,
endless is the victory thou o'er death hast won.

2 Lo! Jesus meets us, risen from the tomb;
lovingly he greets us, scatters fear and gloom;
let the Church with gladness hymns of triumph sing,
for her Lord now liveth; death hath lost its sting.

3 No more we doubt thee, glorious Prince of Life;
life is naught without thee; aid us in our strife;
make us more than conquerors, through thy deathless love;
bring us safe through Jordan to thy home above.

Edmond Budry (1854 – 1932)
tr. R. Birch Hoyle (1875 – 1939)

TUNE (for B♭ instruments)

71

32 Through all our days

Greensleeves   87 87 68 67   *English traditional melody*

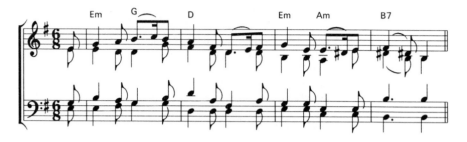

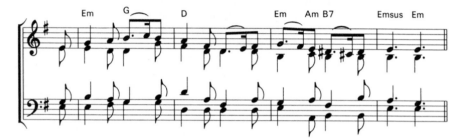

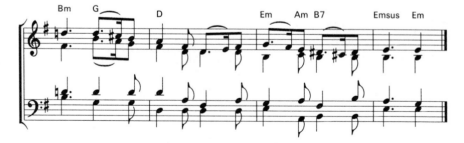

Through all our days we'll sing the praise
of Christ, the resurrected;
who, though divine, did not decline
to be by men afflicted:
pain, pain and suffering—
he knew its taste, he bore its sting;
peace, peace has come to earth
through Christ our King and Saviour.

2   His birth obscure, his family poor,
he owned no crown, no kingdom;
yet those who grieve in fear, believe
since he brought light and freedom:
shame, shame and agony—
though guiltless he of felony;
shout, shout his sinless name,
our Jesus, King and Saviour.

3   At fearful cost his life he lost
that death might be defeated;
the Man of Love, now risen above,
in majesty is seated:
low, low was his descent
to those by sin and sorrow bent;
life, life to all who trust
the Lord, our King and Saviour.

4   And all who trust will find they must
obey the will of heaven;
for grief intense can make some sense
to those who are forgiven:
hard, hard the road he trod—
the Son of Man, the Son of God;
hope, hope in Christ alone,
our reigning King and Saviour.

Michael Saward (b. 1932)

33 Through all the changing scenes of life

Wiltshire 86 86 (CM)   *George Smart (1776–1867)*

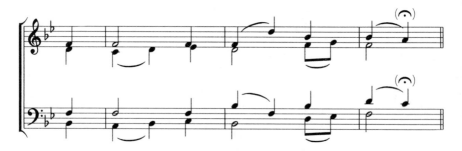

Through all the changing scenes of life,
in trouble and in joy,
the praises of my God shall still
my heart and tongue employ.

2 Of his deliverance I will boast,
till all that are distressed,
from my example comfort take,
and charm their griefs to rest.

3 The hosts of God encamp around
the dwellings of the just;
protection he affords to all
who make his name their trust.

4 O magnify the Lord with me,
with me exalt his name;
when in distress to him I called
he to my rescue came.

5 O make but trial of his love,
experience will decide
how blest are they, and only they,
who in his truth confide.

6 Fear him, you saints, and you will then
have nothing else to fear;
make but his service your delight;
your wants shall be his care.

Nahum Tate (1652–1715)
and Nicholas Brady (1659–1726)
from Psalm 34

34 Amazing grace

Amazing grace 86 86 (CM)

American traditional melody
arr. Helen Killick (b. 1965)

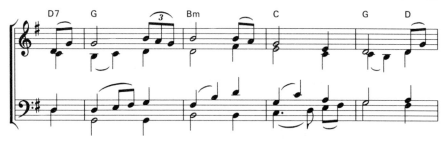

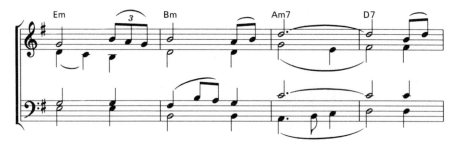

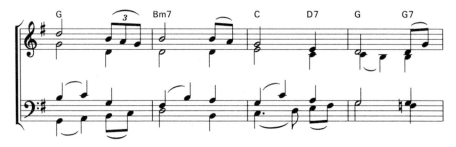

Words © in this version Jubilate Hymns. Arrangement: Presbyterian Church in Ireland/Oxford University Press.

Amazing grace—how sweet the sound—
that saved a wretch like me!
I once was lost, but now am found;
was blind, but now I see.

2　God's grace first taught my heart to fear,
his grace my fears relieved;
how precious did that grace appear
the hour I first believed!

3　Through every danger, trial and snare
I have already come;
his grace has brought me safe thus far,
and grace will lead me home.

4　The Lord has promised good to me,
his word my hope secures;
my shield and stronghold he shall be
as long as life endures.

5　And when this earthly life is past,
and mortal cares shall cease,
I shall possess with Christ at last
eternal joy and peace.

John Newton (1725–1807)
and in this version Jubilate Hymns

35 As the deer

As the deer   *Words and music by Martin Nystrom (b. 1956)*

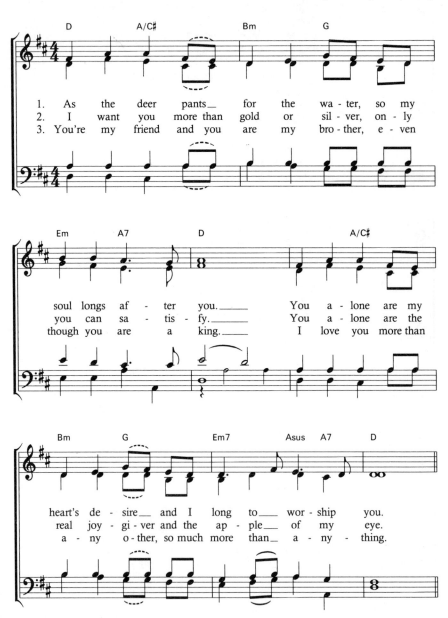

1. As the deer pants for the wa-ter, so my
2. I want you more than gold or sil - ver, on - ly
3. You're my friend and you are my bro-ther, e - ven

soul longs af - ter you. You a - lone are my
you can sa - tis - fy. You a - lone are the
though you are a king. I love you more than

heart's de - sire and I long to wor - ship you.
real joy - gi - ver and the ap - ple of my eye.
a - ny o - ther, so much more than a - ny - thing.

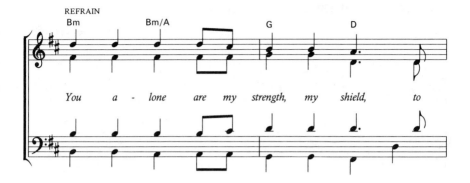

36 As water to the thirsty

Oasis   76 76 66 44 6

T. Brian Coleman (b. 1920)

Words © T. Dudley-Smith. Music © Stainer & Bell Ltd.

As water to the thirsty,
as beauty to the eyes,
as strength that follows weakness,
as truth instead of lies,
as songtime and springtime
and summertime to be,
so is my Lord,
my living Lord,
so is my Lord to me.

2   Like calm in place of clamour,
like peace that follows pain,
like meeting after parting,
like sunshine after rain,
like moonlight and starlight
and sunlight on the sea,
so is my Lord,
my living Lord,
so is my Lord to me.

3   As sleep that follows fever,
as gold instead of grey,
as freedom after bondage,
as sunrise to the day;
as home to the traveller
and all we long to see,
so is my Lord,
my living Lord,
so is my Lord to me.

Timothy Dudley-Smith (b. 1926)

37 Blessed is the man

Blessed is the man

Words and music by Michael Baughen (b. 1930)
Words from Psalm 1
Music arr. Jim Thornton (b. 1947)

GLORY TO GOD

38 Christt be beside me

Bunessan 55 54 D

Scottish traditional melody
arr. Donald Davison (b. 1937)

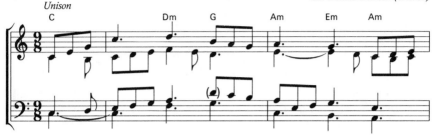

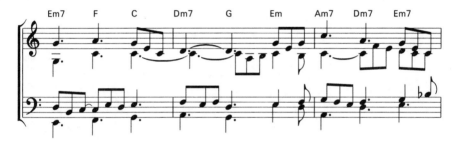

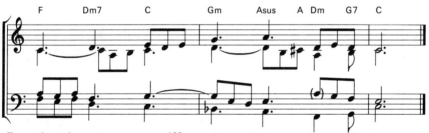

For an alternative arrangement see no. 120.

Christ be beside me,
Christ be before me,
Christ be behind me,
King of my heart.
Christ be within me,
Christ be below me,
Christ be above me,
never to part.

2 Christ on my right hand,
Christ on my left hand,
Christ all around me,
shield in the strife.
Christ in my sleeping,
Christ in my sitting,
Christ in my rising,
light of my life.

3 Christ be in all hearts
thinking about me,
Christ be on all tongues
telling of me.
Christ be the vision
in eyes that see me,
in ears that hear me,
Christ ever be.

James Quinn (b. 1919)
from 'St Patrick's Breastplate'

39 Broken for me

Broken for me

Janet Lunt (b. 1954)
arr. Andrew Maries (b. 1949)

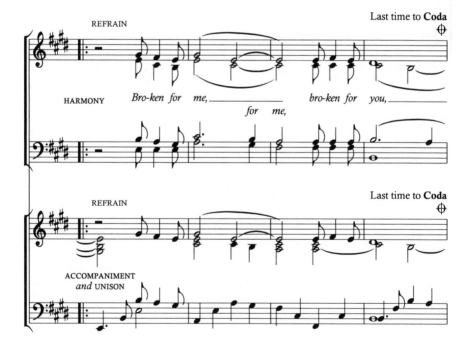

The harmony version may be performed unaccompanied.
Rhythms need to be adjusted to fit the words of verses 2–4.

GLORY TO GOD IN PERSONAL EXPERIENCE

the bo-dy of Je - sus_____ bro-ken for you._____

Je - sus

the bo-dy of Je - sus_____ bro-ken for you.

Je - sus

CODA

(Verses overleaf)

GLORY TO GOD

88

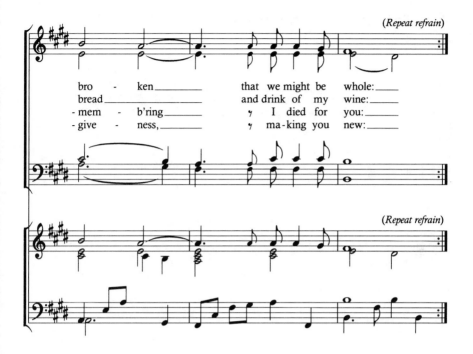

Broken for me, broken for you,
the body of Jesus broken for you.

He offered his body, he poured out his soul,
Jesus was broken that we might be whole:

2 Come to my table and with me dine,
   eat of my bread and drink of my wine:

3 This is my body given for you,
   eat it remembering I died for you:

4 This is my blood I shed for you,
   for your forgiveness, making you new:

Janet Lunt (b. 1954)

40 Father, hear the prayer we offer

Gott will's machen   87 87   *J. L. Steiner (1668–1761)*

Father, hear the prayer we offer—
not for ease our prayer shall be,
but for strength that we may ever
live our lives courageously.

2 Not for ever in green pastures
do we ask our way to be;
but the steep and rugged pathway
may we tread rejoicingly.

3 Not for ever by still waters
would we idly rest and stay;
but would strike the living fountains
from the rocks along our way.

4 Be our strength in hours of weakness,
in our wanderings be our guide;
through endeavour, failure, danger,
Father, be there at our side.

Love M. Willis (1824–1908)

41 Forgive our sins as we forgive

Walsall   86 86 (CM)   *Anchors' Psalmody, c.1721*

'Forgive our sins as we forgive,'
you taught us, Lord, to pray;
but you alone can grant us grace
to live the words we say.

2   How can your pardon reach and bless
the unforgiving heart
that broods on wrongs and will not let
old bitterness depart?

3   In blazing light your cross reveals
the truth we dimly knew:
what trivial debts are owed to us,
how great our debt to you!

4   Lord, cleanse the depths within our souls
and bid resentment cease.
Then, bound to all in bonds of love,
our lives will spread your peace.

Rosamond Herklots (1905–87)

42 Focus my eyes on you

Focus my eyes

Ian White (b. 1956)
arr. Helen Killick (b. 1965)

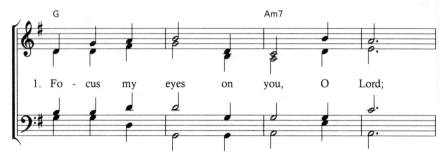

1. Fo - cus my eyes on you, O Lord;

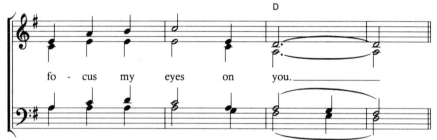

fo - cus my eyes on you. _____

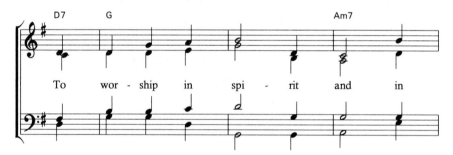

To wor - ship in spi - rit and in

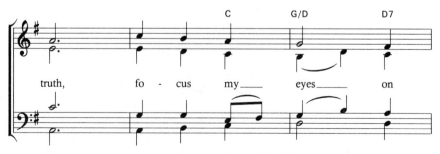

truth, fo - cus my ____ eyes ____ on

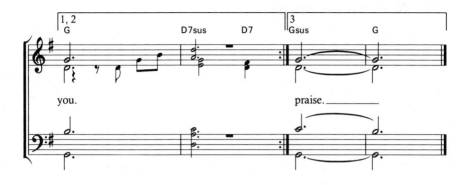

Focus my eyes on you, O Lord;
focus my eyes on you.
To worship in spirit and in truth,
focus my eyes on you.

2   Turn round my life to you, O Lord;
turn round my life to you.
To know from this time you've made me new,
turn round my life to you.

3   Fill up my heart with praise, O Lord;
fill up my heart with praise.
To speak of your love in every place,
fill up my heart with praise.

Ian White (b. 1956)

43 God, be merciful to me

Aberystwyth   77 77 D   *Joseph Parry (1841–1903)*

God, be merciful to me,
let your love my refuge be;
my offences wash away,
cleanse me from my sin today.
My transgressions I confess,
grief and guilt my soul oppress;
I have sinned against your grace
and provoked you to your face.

2 Wash me, wash me pure within,
cleanse, O cleanse me from my sin;
in your righteousness I trust,
in your judgements you are just.
Come, salvation to impart,
teach your wisdom to my heart;
make me pure, your grace bestow,
that your mercy I may know.

3 Gracious God, my heart renew,
make my spirit right and true;
from my sins O hide your face,
blot them out in boundless grace.
Cast your servant not away,
let your Spirit with me stay;
make me joyful, willing, strong,
teach me your salvation's song!

Paraphrased from Psalm 51
by 'Word & Music'

44   He lives in us, the Christ of God

Kingsfold   86 86 D (DCM)

English traditional melody
arr. Ralph Vaughan Williams (1872–1958)

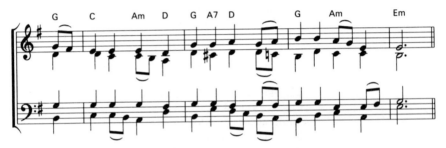

He lives in us, the Christ of God,
his Spirit joins with ours;
he brings to us the Father's grace
with powers beyond our powers.
And if enticing sin grows strong,
when human nature fails,
God's Spirit in our inner self
fights with us, and prevails.

2   Our pangs of guilt and fears of death
are Satan's stratagems—
by Jesus Christ who died for us
God pardons; who condemns?
And when we cannot feel our faith,
nor bring ourselves to pray,
the Spirit pleads with God for us
in words we could not say.

3   God gave his Son to save us all—
no greater love is known!
And shall that love abandon us
who have become Christ's own?
For God has raised him from the grave,
in this we stand assured;
so none can tear us from the love
of Jesus Christ our Lord.

Michael Perry (b. 1942)
from Romans 8

45 How can we sing with joy to God

Billing   86 86 (CM)

Richard Terry (1865–1938)

Alternative tune: JACKSON, *Church Hymnary: Third Edition* no. 565, *Revised Church Hymnary* no. 507

How can we sing with joy to God,
how can we pray to him,
when we are far away from God
in selfishness and sin?

2   How can we claim to do God's will
when we have turned away
from things of God to things of earth,
and willed to disobey?

3   How can we praise the love of God
which all his works make known,
when all our works turn from his love
to choices of our own?

4   God knows the sinful things we do,
the Godless life we live,
yet in his love he calls to us,
so ready to forgive.

5   So we will turn again to God—
his ways will be our ways,
his will our will, his love our love,
and he himself our praise!

Brian Foley (b. 1919)

46 I can talk to God

Talking to God   55 55 77 74   *Eric H. Swinstead (1881–1950)*

Unison

I can talk to God,
he will hear my prayers.
I can talk to God,
for I know he cares.
He will listen when I say,
'Thank you for your love today,
for your help in every way,
Oh, thank you, God.'

2 I can talk to God,
he will hear my prayers.
I can talk to God,
for I know he cares.
He will listen when I say,
'I have done wrong things today,
please forgive me now I pray,
forgive me, God.'

3 I can talk to God,
he will hear my prayers.
I can talk to God,
for I know he cares.
He will listen when I say,
'Please help all my friends today,
help them in their work and play,
please help them, God.'

J. Sibley

47 I lift my eyes to the quiet hills

Davos

Michael Baughen (b. 1930)

1. I lift my eyes to the qui-et hills in the press of a bu-sy day; as green hills stand in a dus-ty land so God is my strength and stay.

I lift my eyes
to the quiet hills
in the press of a busy day;
as green hills stand
in a dusty land
so God is my strength and stay.

2   I lift my eyes
to the quiet hills
to a calm that is mine to share;
secure and still
in the Father's will
and kept by the Father's care.

3   I lift my eyes
to the quiet hills
with a prayer as I turn to sleep;
by day, by night,
through the dark and light
my Shepherd will guard his sheep.

4   I lift my eyes
to the quiet hills
and my heart to the Father's throne;
in all my ways
to the end of days
the Lord will preserve his own.

Timothy Dudley-Smith (b. 1926)

48 I'll love the Lord

MacDowell

John Bell (b. 1949)
arr. Helen Killick (b. 1965)

GLORY TO GOD

- side_ me,____ I'll love the Lord with bo - dy, soul and mind.____
- fore_ me,____ I'll give my yes to him who gave me all.____
Spi - rit,____ to make me new and set my faith on fire.____

(Cantor/Choir) 1 & 4 *I'll love the Lord with all that lies inside me,*
I'll love the Lord with body, soul and mind.

(All) I'll love the Lord with all that lies inside me,
I'll love the Lord with body, soul and mind.

(Cantor/Choir) *And every goodness, every blessing in the Lord I'll find.*

(All) And every goodness, every blessing in the Lord I'll find.
I'll love the Lord with all that lies inside me,
I'll love the Lord with body, soul and mind.

(etc.) 2 *I'll walk the path that Christ has walked before me,*
I'll give my yes to him who gave me all.
I'll walk the path that Christ has walked before me,
I'll give my yes to him who gave me all.
In every sound and every silence I will hear his call.
In every sound and every silence I will hear his call.
I'll walk the path that Christ has walked before me,
I'll give my yes to him who gave me all.

3 *I'll let my life be open to God's Spirit,*
to make me new and set my faith on fire.
I'll let my life be open to God's Spirit,
to make me new and set my faith on fire.
More than all things his peace and presence are what I desire.
More than all things his peace and presence are what I desire.
I'll let my life be open to God's Spirit,
to make me new and set my faith on fire.

John Bell (b. 1949)
Graham Maule (b. 1958)

49 I, the Lord of sea and sky

Here I am, Lord

Daniel Schutte, SJ
arr. Oxford University Press

I, the Lord of sea and sky,
I have heard my people cry.
All who dwell in dark or sin
My hand will save.
I, who made the stars of night,
I will make their darkness bright.
Who will bear my light to them?
Whom shall I send?

Here I am, Lord.
Is it I, Lord?
I have heard you calling in the night.
I will go, Lord,
if you lead me.
I will hold your people in my heart.

2 I, the Lord of snow and rain,
   I have borne my people's pain.
   I have wept for love of them.
   They turn away.
   I will break their hearts of stone,
   give them hearts for love alone.
   I will speak my word to them.
   Whom shall I send?

3 I, the Lord of wind and flame,
   I will tend the poor and lame.
   I will set a feast for them.
   My hand will save.
   Finest bread I will provide
   till their hearts be satisfied.
   I will give my life to them.
   Whom shall I send?

Daniel Schutte, SJ

50 In the morning when I rise

God is near 777 3

Phil Burt (b. 1957)
arr. Helen Killick (b. 1965)

1. In the morn-ing when I rise, (*in the morn-ing when I rise,*) when I o-pen up my eyes, (*when I o-pen up my eyes,*) rain or shine or cold and ice, (*rain or shine or cold and ice,*) God is near.

2 When I help and when I play,
he is there to show the way,
close beside me all the day,
God is near.

3 Then when I turn off the light,
when I go to sleep at night,
I am always in his sight,
God is near.

Marjorie Anderson

51 Lord, you have searched

Winscott   88 88 (LM)   *Samuel S. Wesley (1810–76)*

Lord, you have searched and known my ways
and understood my thought from far;
how can I rightly sound your praise
or tell how great your wonders are?

2 Besetting me, before, behind,
upon my life your hand is laid;
caught in the compass of your mind
are all the things that you have made.

3 Such knowledge is too wonderful,
too high for me to understand—
enough that the Unsearchable
has searched my heart and held my hand.

Peter Jarvis (b. 1925)
from Psalm 139: 1–6

52 Look and learn

Look and learn   99 99 77 77

Nah Young-Soo
arr. Iona Community

1. Look and learn from the birds of the air, fly - ing high a-bove wor - ry and fear; nei - ther sow - ing nor har - vest-ing seed, yet they're gi - ven what - e - ver they need. If the God of earth and heav'n cares for birds as

much— as this, won't he care— much more— for you, if you put_____ your trust_____ in him?

Look and learn from the birds of the air,
flying high above worry and fear;
neither sowing nor harvesting seed,
yet they're given whatever they need.
If the God of earth and heaven
cares for birds as much as this,
won't he care much more for you,
if you put your trust in him?

2 Look and learn from the flowers of the field,
bringing beauty and colour to life;
neither sewing nor tailoring cloth,
yet they're dressed in the finest attire.
If the God of earth and heaven
cares for flowers as much as this,
won't he care much more for you
if you put your trust in him?

3 What God wants should be our will;
where God calls should be our goal.
When we seek the kingdom first,
all we've lost is ours again.
Let's be done with anxious thoughts,
set aside tomorrow's cares,
live each day that God provides
putting all our trust in him.

Iona Community
from Matthew 6: 23–4

53 Living Lord

Living Lord   98 88 83   *Patrick Appleford (b. 1925)*

1. Lord Je-sus Christ, you have come to us,

you are one with us, Ma-ry's son;

clean-sing our souls from all their sin, pour-ing your love and

good-ness in: Je-sus, our love for you we sing— li - ving

Lord Jesus Christ, you have come to us,
you are one with us, Mary's son;
cleansing our souls from all their sin,
pouring your love and goodness in:
Jesus, our love for you we sing—
living Lord!

2 Lord Jesus Christ, you have come to us,
born as one of us, Mary's son;
led out to die on Calvary,
risen from death to set us free:
living Lord Jesus, help us see
you are Lord!

3 Lord Jesus Christ, I would come to you,
live my life for you, Son of God;
all your commands I know are true,
your many gifts will make me new:
into my life your power breaks through—
living Lord!

At communion, this may be sung:

4 Lord Jesus Christ, now and every day
teach us how to pray, Son of God;
you have commanded us to do
this in remembrance, Lord, of you:
into our lives your power breaks through—
living Lord!

Patrick Appleford (b. 1925)

(harmony version overleaf)

Harmony

1. Lord Je - sus Christ,_____ you_____ have come to us,

you_____ are one with us, Ma - ry's son;_____

clean-sing our souls_ from all their sin, pour-ing your love_ and

good-ness in: Je-sus, our love for you we sing— li - ving_

Lord Jesus Christ, you have come to us,
you are one with us, Mary's son;
cleansing our souls from all their sin,
pouring your love and goodness in:
Jesus, our love for you we sing—
living Lord!

2   Lord Jesus Christ, you have come to us,
born as one of us, Mary's son;
led out to die on Calvary,
risen from death to set us free:
living Lord Jesus, help us see
you are Lord!

3   Lord Jesus Christ, I would come to you,
live my life for you, Son of God;
all your commands I know are true,
your many gifts will make me new:
into my life your power breaks through—
living Lord!

At communion, this may be sung:

4   Lord Jesus Christ, now and every day
teach us how to pray, Son of God;
you have commanded us to do
this in remembrance, Lord, of you:
into our lives your power breaks through—
living Lord!

Patrick Appleford (b. 1925)

54 Lord, will you turn from your anger

Langleigh 11 10 11 10

Kenneth W. Coates (b. 1917)

Lord, will you turn from your anger and hear me?
Guilt and remorse are the burdens I bear;
when I acknowledge my sin and my folly,
show your compassion, your love and your care.

2 Lord, though my friends and companions desert me,
you will not leave me—I know you are near.
Hear my deep sighing, and see my great sorrow—
you know each secret, each longing, each fear.

3 Lord, will you answer with words of forgiveness?
Then shall my joy and my peace be restored:
faithful Redeemer and God of all comfort,
you are my Saviour, my King and my Lord!

Mollie Knight (1917–93)
from Psalm 38

55 My Lord, what love is this

Amazing love

Words and music by
Graham Kendrick (b. 1950)

INTRODUCTION
Unison

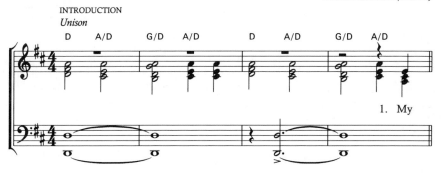

Lord, _____ what love is this _____ that
(2.) so, _____ they watched him die, _____ des -
(3.) now _____ this love of Christ ____ shall

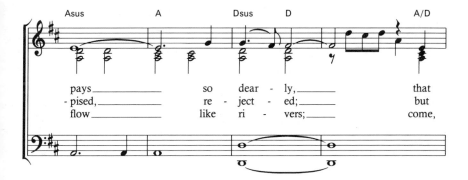

pays _____ so dear - ly, _____ that
- pised, _____ re - ject - ed; _____ but
flow _____ like ri - vers; _____ come,

GLORY TO GOD

I,_____ the guil-ty one,_____ may
O,_____ the blood he shed_____ flowed
wash_____ your guilt a-way,_____ live

go free!_____
for me!_____
a - gain!_____

REFRAIN

A - ma-zing love,_____

O what sac-ri-fice,_____ the Son of God_____

given for me._____ My debt he pays_____

_____ and my death he dies, _____ that I_____

_____ might live, _____ that I_____ might

live. _____

2. And
3. And _____ might

live, _____ that I_____ might live.

56 Make me a channel of your peace

St Francis

Words and music by Sebastian Temple (b. 1928)
Words from the prayer of St Francis
Music arr. John Barnard (b. 1948)

1. Make me a chan-nel of your peace: where there is hat-red let me bring your love, where there is in-ju-ry, your par-don, Lord, and

2. Make me a chan-nel of your peace: where there's des-pair in life let me bring hope, where there is dark-ness, on - ly light, and

3. Make me a chan-nel of your peace: it is in par-don-ing that we are par - doned, in gi-ving of our-selves that we re - ceive, and in

Dedicated to Mrs Frances Tracy.

57 O God of faith

O waly waly   88 88 (LM)

Traditional English melody
arr. Helen Killick (b. 1965)

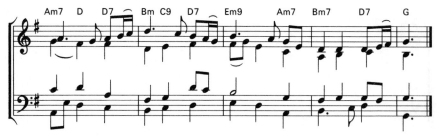

O God of faith, help me believe.
Help me to know you shelter me,
and though your face I cannot see,
O may I feel your strength in me.

2 O God of hope, help me to know
that hope in you is strong and sure,
that you raised Jesus from the grave,
and hope is in your power to save.

3 O God of love, help me to see
that love sent Christ to die for me,
and though unworthy I can say
that love endures from day to day.

4 O God of faith, help me believe,
O God of hope, my Saviour be.
O God of love, show love through me,
and shine for all the world to see.

Ron Hopgood

58 Speak, Lord, in the stillness

Quietude 65 65

Harold Green (1871–1930)

Speak, Lord, in the stillness,
speak your word to me;
help me now to listen
in expectancy.

2 Speak, O gracious Master,
in this quiet hour;
let me see your face, Lord,
feel your touch of power.

3 For the words you give me,
they are life indeed;
living bread from heaven,
now my spirit feed.

4 Speak, your servant listens—
I await your word;
let me know your presence,
let your voice be heard!

5 Fill me with the knowledge
of your glorious will;
all your own good pleasure
in my life fulfil.

Emily Crawford (1864–1927)
and in this version Jubilate Hymns

59 O Master Christ

Repton   86 88 6 extended

Charles H. Parry (1848–1918)

O Master Christ, draw near to take
your undisputed place;
my gifts and faculties remake,
form and re-fashion for your sake
an instrument of peace.

2   O Master Christ, I choose to sow
in place of hatred, love;
where wounds and injuries are now
may healing and forgiveness grow
as gifts from God above.

3   O Master Christ, I choose to plant
hope where there is despair;
a warmth of joy, a shaft of light
where darkness has diminished sight,
where sorrow leaves its scar.

4   O Master Christ, make this my goal—
less to receive than give;
to sympathise—and to make whole,
to understand and to console
and so, through death, to live.

David Mowbray (b. 1938)
from the Prayer of St Francis

60 One more step along the world I go

Southcote   99 79 with refrain

Sydney Carter (b. 1915)

REFRAIN

And it's   from   the   old   I   tra - vel   to   the   new. ___

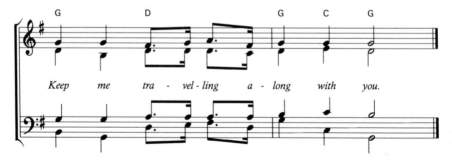

Keep   me   tra - vel - ling   a - long   with   you.

Words & music © Stainer & Bell Ltd.

One more step along the world I go,
one more step along the world I go.
From the old things to the new
keep me travelling along with you.

>   *And it's from the old I travel to the new.*
>   *Keep me travelling along with you.*

2   Round the corner of the world I turn,
more and more about the world I learn.
All the new things that I see
you'll be looking at along with me.

3   As I travel through the bad and good
keep me travelling the way I should.
Where I see no way to go
you'll be telling me the way, I know.

4   Give me courage when the world is rough,
keep me loving though the world is tough.
Leap and sing in all I do,
keep me travelling along with you.

5   You are older than the world can be,
you are younger than the life in me.
Ever old and ever new,
keep me travelling along with you.

Sydney Carter (b. 1915)

61 Safe in the shadow of the Lord

Creator God   86 86 (CM)   *Norman Warren (b. 1934)*

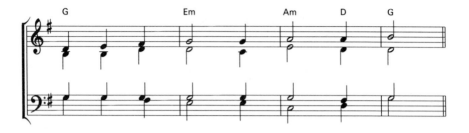

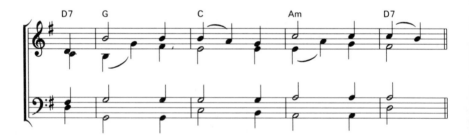

Safe in the shadow of the Lord
beneath his hand and power,
I trust in him,
I trust in him,
my fortress and my tower.

2   My hope is set on God alone
though Satan spreads his snare,
I trust in him,
I trust in him,
to keep me in his care.

3   From fears and phantoms of the night,
from foes about my way,
I trust in him,
I trust in him,
by darkness as by day.

4   His holy angels keep my feet
secure from every stone;
I trust in him,
I trust in him,
and unafraid go on.

5   Strong in the Everlasting Name,
and in my Father's care,
I trust in him,
I trust in him,
who hears and answers prayer.

6   Safe in the shadow of the Lord,
possessed by love divine,
I trust in him,
I trust in him,
and meet his love with mine.

Timothy Dudley-Smith (b. 1926)
from Psalm 91

62 Spirit of holiness

Blow the wind southerly   12 10 12 10 12 11 12 11

Traditional English melody
arr. John Barnard (b. 1948)

REFRAIN
Unison

Spi - rit of ho - li - ness, wis - dom and faith - ful - ness, wind of the

Lord, blow-ing strong-ly and free: strength of our ser-ving and joy of our

Fine

wor - ship - ping— Spi - rit of God, bring your full - ness to me!

VERSE
Harmony

Spirit of holiness, wisdom and faithfulness,
wind of the Lord, blowing strongly and free:
strength of our serving and joy of our worshipping—
Spirit of God, bring your fullness to me!

You came to interpret and teach us effectively
all that the Saviour has spoken and done;
to glorify Jesus is all your activity—
promise and gift of the Father and Son:

2 You came with your gifts to supply all our poverty,
   pouring your love on the Church in her need;
   you came with your fruit for our growth to maturity,
   richly refreshing the souls that you feed:

Christopher Idle (b. 1938)

63 Sweet is the work

Deep harmony   88 88 (LM)   *Handel Parker (1854–1928)*

Sweet is the work, my God, my King,
to praise your name, give thanks and sing;
to show your love by morning light,
and talk of all your truth at night.

2 Sweet is the day, the first and best,
on which I share your sacred rest;
so let my heart in tune be found,
like David's harp of joyful sound.

3 My heart shall triumph in the Lord
and bless his works, and bless his word:
God's works of grace, how bright they shine—
how deep his counsels, how divine!

4 Soon I shall see and hear and know
all I desired on earth below,
and all my powers for God employ
in that eternal world of joy.

Isaac Watts (1674–1748)

64 There are hundreds of sparrows

There are hundreds of sparrows   11 12 12 10   *John Larsson (b. 1938)*

There are hundreds of sparrows, thousands, millions,
they're two a penny, far too many there must be;
there are hundreds and thousands, millions of sparrows,
but God knows every one and God knows me.

2   There are hundreds of flowers, thousands, millions,
and flowers fair the meadows wear for all to see;
there are hundreds and thousands, millions of flowers,
but God knows every one and God knows me.

3   There are hundreds of planets, thousands, millions,
way out in space each has a place by God's decree;
there are hundreds and thousands, millions of planets,
but God knows every one and God knows me.

4   There are hundreds of children, thousands, millions,
and yet their names are written on God's memory;
there are hundreds and thousands, millions of children,
but God knows every one and God knows me.

John Gowans (b. 1934)

65 Take this moment

Take this moment   75 75

John Bell (b. 1949)

1. Take this mo - ment, sign__ and__ space;

take my friends a - round;_____

here a - mong us__ make_ the__ place

GLORY TO GOD IN PERSONAL EXPERIENCE

where your love is found.

Take this moment, sign and space;
take my friends around;
here among us make the place
where your love is found.

2   Take the time to call my name,
    take the time to mend
    who I am and what I've been,
    all I've failed to tend.

3   Take the tiredness of my days,
    take my past regret,
    letting your forgiveness touch
    all I can't forget.

4   Take the little child in me,
    scared of growing old;
    help me here to find my worth
    made in Christ's own mould.

5   Take my talents, take my skills,
    take what's yet to be;
    let my life be yours, and yet,
    let it still be me.

John Bell (b. 1949)
Graham Maule (b. 1958)

137

66 Talk to God and share with him

All things bright and beautiful   76 76 D   William Monk (1823–89)

REFRAIN
Unison

Talk to God and share with him the thoughts you have each day.

Let him know what's on your mind—he loves to hear you pray.

VERSE
Harmony

1. With 'Sor - ry', 'Please' and 'Thank_____ you', there's
2. In a - ny place you go_____ to our

such a___ lot to say._____ God loves to hear you
Fa - ther,_ God is there;_____ he knows what you are

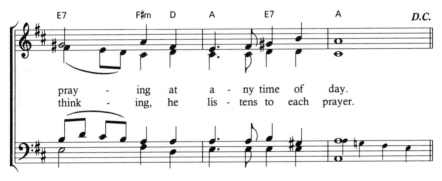

D.C.

pray - ing at a - ny time of day.
think - ing, he lis - tens to each prayer.

Talk to God and share with him
the thoughts you have each day.
Let him know what's on your mind—
he loves to hear you pray.

With 'Sorry', 'Please' and 'Thank you',
there's such a lot to say.
God loves to hear you praying
at any time of day.

2 In any place you go to
our Father, God, is there;
he knows what you are thinking,
he listens to each prayer.

Margaret Old (b. 1932)

67 The journey of life

Follow my leader

Valerie Collison (b. 1933)

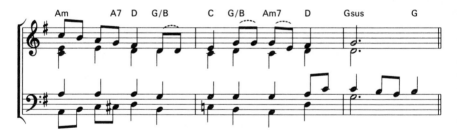

Will you ride, ride, ride with the King of kings, will you

GLORY TO GOD IN PERSONAL EXPERIENCE

fol-low my lea - der true;____ will you shout ho - san-na to the low - ly Son of God, who died for__ me__ and you?

The journey of life may be easy, may be hard,
there'll be dangers on the way;
with Christ at my side I'll do battle as I ride
'gainst the foe that would lead me astray.

*Will you ride, ride, ride with the King of kings,
will you follow my leader true;
will you shout hosanna to the lowly Son of God,
who died for me and you?*

2 My burden is light and a song is in my heart,
as I travel on life's way;
for Christ is my Lord and he's given me his word,
that by my side he'll stay.

3 When doubts arise and when tears are in my eyes,
when all seems lost to me,
with Christ as my guide I can smile whate'er betide,
for he my strength will be.

4 I'll follow my leader wherever he may go,
for Jesus is my friend;
he'll lead me on to the place where he has gone,
when I come to my journey's end.

Valerie Collison (b. 1933)

68 Today I awake

Slithers of gold   11 10 11 10   *John Bell (b. 1949)*

1. To-day I a-wake___ and God is be-fore___ me. At

night, as I dreamt,___ he sum-moned the day;___ for

God ne-ver sleeps___ but pat-terns the morn - ing with

sli-thers of gold___ or glo-ry in grey.___

Today I awake
and God is before me.
At night, as I dreamt,
he summoned the day;
for God never sleeps
but patterns the morning
with slithers of gold
or glory in grey.

2 Today I arise
and Christ is beside me.
He walked through the dark
to scatter new light.
Yes, Christ is alive,
and beckons his people
to hope and to heal,
resist and invite.

3 Today I affirm
the Spirit within me
at worship and work,
in struggle and rest.
The Spirit inspires
all life which is changing
from fearing to faith,
from broken to blest.

4 Today I enjoy
the Trinity round me,
above and beneath,
before and behind;
the Maker, the Son,
the Spirit together—
they called me to life
and call me their friend.

John Bell (b. 1949)
Graham Maule (b. 1958)

69 What a friend we have in Jesus

FIRST TUNE

Manor House   87 87 D

Frederick Carter (b. 1913)

Music © F. G. Carter.

What a friend we have in Jesus,
all our sins and griefs to bear;
what a privilege to carry
everything to God in prayer!
O what peace we often forfeit,
O what needless pain we bear,
all because we do not carry
everything to God in prayer.

2 Have we trials and temptations,
is there trouble anywhere?
We should never be discouraged:
take it to the Lord in prayer.
Can we find a friend so faithful
who will all our sorrows share?
Jesus knows our every weakness—
take it to the Lord in prayer.

3 Are we weak and heavy-laden,
burdened with a load of care?
Jesus is our mighty Saviour:
he will listen to our prayer.
Do your friends despise, forsake you?
Take it to the Lord in prayer;
in his arms he will enfold you
and his love will shield you there.

Joseph Scriven (1819–86)

(69) What a friend we have in Jesus

SECOND TUNE

Converse   87 87 D   *Charles Converse (1832–1918)*

What a friend we have in Jesus,
all our sins and griefs to bear;
what a privilege to carry
everything to God in prayer!
O what peace we often forfeit,
O what needless pain we bear,
all because we do not carry
everything to God in prayer.

2 Have we trials and temptations,
is there trouble anywhere?
We should never be discouraged:
take it to the Lord in prayer.
Can we find a friend so faithful
who will all our sorrows share?
Jesus knows our every weakness—
take it to the Lord in prayer.

3 Are we weak and heavy-laden,
burdened with a load of care?
Jesus is our mighty Saviour:
he will listen to our prayer.
Do your friends despise, forsake you?
Take it to the Lord in prayer;
in his arms he will enfold you
and his love will shield you there.

Joseph Scriven (1819–86)

70 The Summons

Kelvingrove   76 76 77 76

Scottish traditional melody
arr. Oxford University Press

1. Will you come and fol-low me if I but call your name?___ Will you go where you don't know and ne-ver be the same?___ Will you let my love be shown,___ will you let my name be known,___ will you

let my life be grown in you and you in me?____

Will you come and follow me
if I but call your name?
Will you go where you don't know
and never be the same?
Will you let my love be shown,
will you let my name be known,
will you let my life be grown
in you and you in me?

2 Will you leave yourself behind
if I but call your name?
Will you care for cruel and kind
and never be the same?
Will you risk the hostile stare
should your life attract or scare?
Will you let me answer prayer
in you and you in me?

3 Will you let the blinded see
if I but call your name?
Will you set the prisoners free
and never be the same?
Will you kiss the leper clean,
and do such as this unseen,
and admit to what I mean
in you and you in me?

4 Will you love the 'you' you hide
if I but call your name?
Will you quell the fear inside
and never be the same?
Will you use the faith you've found
to reshape the world around,
through my sight and touch and sound
in you and you in me?

5 Lord, your summons echoes true
when you but call my name.
Let me turn and follow you
and never be the same.
In your company I'll go
where your love and footsteps show.
Thus I'll move and live and grow
in you and you in me.

John Bell (b. 1949)
Graham Maule (b. 1958)

71 Thuma mina

Thuma mina

South African traditional
arr. Anders Nyberg

CANTOR

1. Thu - ma mi-na.*

ALL

1. & 5. Thu-ma mi-na, thu-ma mi-na, thu-ma
(2.) Je-sus, send me, Je-sus, send me,
(3.) Je-sus, lead me, Je-sus, lead me,
(4.) Je-sus, fill me, Je-sus, fill me,

1–4 | Last time

2. Send me,— Lord.
3. Lead me,— Lord.
4. Fill me,— Lord.
5. Thu - ma mi - na.

mi - na so - man - dla.   2. Send me, - dla.
Je - sus, send me, Lord.   3. Lead me,
Je - sus, lead me, Lord.   4. Fill me,
Je - sus, fill me, Lord.   5. Thu - ma

*Pronounced 'Tooma meena'.
This song is best sung unaccompanied, in harmony.

72 Christ is our cornerstone

Harewood   66 66 88   *Samuel S. Wesley (1810–76)*

Alternative tune: DARWALL'S 148TH, *Church Hymnary: Third Edition* no. 296,
Revised Church Hymnary no. 135

Christ is our cornerstone,
on him alone we build;
with his true saints alone
the courts of heaven are filled;
   on his great love
   our hopes we place
   of present grace
   and joys above.

2 With psalms and hymns of praise
this holy place shall ring;
our voices we will raise,
the Three-in-One to sing;
   and thus proclaim
   in joyful song
   both loud and long,
   that glorious name.

3 Here, gracious God, draw near
as in your name we bow;
each true petition hear,
accept each faithful vow;
   and more and more
   on all who pray
   each holy day
   your blessings pour.

4 Here may we gain from heaven
the grace which we implore;
and may that grace, once given,
be with us evermore,
   until that day
   when all the blessed
   to endless rest
   are called away.

John Chandler (1806–76)
from the Latin (c. 7th century)

73 Bless and keep us, Lord

Komm, Herr, segne uns   11 11 5 66 5

Melody by Dieter Trautwein (b. 1928)
harm. the compilers of 'Rejoice and Sing' (1991)

Bless and keep us, Lord, in your love united,
from your family never separated.
You make all things new
as we follow after;
whether tears or laughter,
we belong to you.

2   Blessing shrivels up when your children hoard it;
help us, Lord, to share, for we can afford it:
blessing only grows
in the act of sharing,
in a life of caring,
love that heals and glows.

3   Fill your world with peace, such as you intended.
Teach us prize the earth, love, replenish, tend it.
Lord, uplift, fulfil
all who sow in sadness:
let them reap with gladness,
by your kingdom thrilled.

4   You renew our life, changing tears to laughter;
we belong to you, so we follow after.
Bless and keep us, Lord,
in your love united,
never separated
from your living Word.

Dieter Trautwein (b. 1928)
tr. Fred Kaan (b. 1929)

74 Christ our King

Sunderland   87 87 D

Geoffrey Beaumont (1903–70)

Words & music © 1960 Josef Weinberger Ltd.

Christ our King in glory reigning,
all our strength from you proceeds;
born of Mary, not disdaining
work or pain to share our needs;
you have conquered sin's infection,
guiltless victim for us killed,
by your mighty resurrection,
Christ in us your Church rebuild.

2 Lord, look down in your compassion,
free your people from their sin;
only by your cross and Passion
may we rise renewed within;
make us honest in our living,
with your grace may we be filled;
by your love and free forgiving,
Christ in us your Church rebuild.

3 Lord, to everyone supplying
different gifts for all to use;
give us strength, on you relying,
all our selfishness to lose.
May we each in our vocation
with your Spirit be instilled;
by your humble incarnation,
Christ in us your Church rebuild.

4 Lord, you call us all to witness
by our worship and our love;
Lord, look not on our unfitness,
send your Spirit from above;
Jesus, humbly we adore you,
make us yours as you have willed,
by your reign of endless glory,
Christ in us your Church rebuild.

Patrick Appleford (b. 1925)

75 Church of God, elect and glorious

Lux Eoi   87 87 D   *Arthur Sullivan (1842–1900)*

Church of God, elect and glorious,
holy nation, chosen race;
called as God's own special people,
royal priests and heirs of grace:
know the purpose of your calling,
show to all his mighty deeds;
tell of love which knows no limits,
grace which meets all human needs.

2 God has called you out of darkness
into his most marvellous light;
brought his truth to life within you,
turned your blindness into sight.
Let your light so shine around you
that God's name is glorified;
and all find fresh hope and purpose
in Christ Jesus crucified.

3 Once you were an alien people,
strangers to God's heart of love;
but he brought you home in mercy,
citizens of heaven above.
Let his love flow out to others,
let them feel a Father's care;
that they too may know his welcome
and his countless blessings share.

4 Church of God, elect and holy,
be the people he intends;
strong in faith and swift to answer
each command your master sends:
royal priests, fulfil your calling
through your sacrifice and prayer;
give your lives in joyful service,
sing his praise, his love declare.

James Seddon (1915–83)
from 1 Peter 2: 9–11

76 Day is done

Ar hyd y nos   84 84 88 84

Welsh traditional melody
arr. John Barnard (b. 1948)

Words © 1969, 1985 James Quinn, SJ. Printed by permission of Geoffrey Chapman, a division of Cassell plc.
Arrangement © J. Barnard/Jubilate Hymns.

Day is done, but Love unfailing
dwells ever here;
shadows fall, but hope, prevailing,
calms every fear.
Loving Father, none forsaking,
take our hearts, of Love's own making,
watch our sleeping, guard our waking,
be always near!

2   Dark descends, but Light unending,
shines through our night;
you are with us, ever lending
new strength to sight;
one in love, your truth confessing,
one in hope of heaven's blessing,
may we see, in love's possessing,
love's endless light!

3   Eyes will close, but you, unsleeping,
watch by our side;
death may come: in love's safe keeping
still we abide.
God of love, all evil quelling,
sin forgiving, fear dispelling,
stay with us, our hearts indwelling,
this eventide!

James Quinn (b. 1919)

77 Deep in the shadows of the past

Northover   86 86 D (DCM)   *Peter Cutts (b. 1937)*

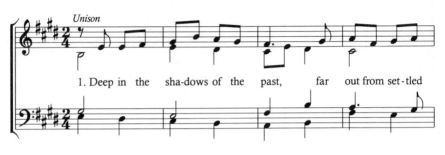

1. Deep in the sha-dows of the past,   far   out from set-tled

lands,   some no - mads tra - velled with their

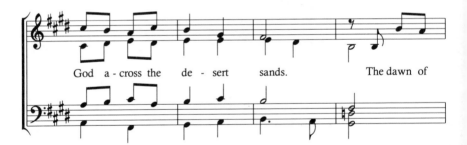

God a - cross the   de - sert   sands.   The dawn of

hope for hu-man-kind was glimpsed by   them a - lone: a

pro-mise call-ing them a - head, a fu-ture yet un - known.

Alternative tune: KINGSFOLD, no. 44

Deep in the shadows of the past,
far out from settled lands,
some nomads travelled with their God
across the desert sands.
The dawn of hope for humankind
was glimpsed by them alone:
a promise calling them ahead,
a future yet unknown.

2   While others bowed to changeless gods
they met a mystery:
God with an uncompleted name,
'I am what I will be';
and by their tents, around their fires,
in story, song and law
they praised, remembered, handed on
a past that promised more.

3   From Abraham to Nazareth
the promise changed and grew,
while some, remembering the past,
recorded what they knew,
and some, in letters or laments,
in prophecy and praise,
recovered, held, and re-expressed
new hope for changing days.

4   For all the writings that survived,
for leaders, long ago,
who sifted, chose, and then preserved
the Bible that we know,
give thanks, and find its promise yet
our comfort, strength, and call,
the working model for our faith,
alive with hope for all.

Brian Wren (b. 1936)

161

78 Freedom and life are ours

From strength to strength   66 86 D (DSM)   *Edward Naylor (1867–1934)*

Words © C. Idle/Jubilate Hymns.

Freedom and life are ours
for Christ has set us free!
Never again submit to powers
that lead to slavery:
Christ is the Lord who breaks
our chains, our bondage ends,
Christ is the rescuer who makes
the helpless slaves his friends.

2   Called by the Lord to use
our freedom and be strong,
not letting liberty excuse
a life of blatant wrong:
freed from the law's stern hand
God's gift of grace to prove,
know that the law's entire demand
is gladly met by love.

3   Spirit of God, come, fill,
emancipate us all!
Speak to us, Word of truth, until
before his throne we fall:
glory and liberty
our Father has decreed,
and if the Son shall make us free
we shall be free indeed!

Christopher Idle (b. 1938)

79 From heaven you came, helpless babe

The Servant King   *Graham Kendrick (b. 1950)*

1. From heav'n you came, help-less babe, en-tered our world, your
glo - ry veiled; not to be served but to serve,
and give your life that we might live.

REFRAIN

This is our God,_____ the Ser-vant King,_____ he calls us

now to fol - low him,_____ to bring our lives as a dai - ly of - fer - ing_____ of wor - ship to_____ the Ser - vant King. King.

From heaven you came, helpless babe,
entered our world, your glory veiled;
not to be served but to serve,
and give your life that we might live.

This is our God, the Servant King,
he calls us now to follow him,
to bring our lives as a daily offering
of worship to the Servant King.

2   There in the garden of tears,
    my heavy load he chose to bear;
    his heart with sorrow was torn,
    'Yet not my will but yours,' he said.

3   Come see his hands and his feet,
    the scars that speak of sacrifice,
    hands that flung stars into space
    to cruel nails surrendered.

4   So let us learn how to serve,
    and in our lives enthrone him;
    each other's needs to prefer,
    for it is Christ we're serving.

Graham Kendrick (b. 1950)

80 Go forth and tell!

Yanworth   10 10 10 10   *John Barnard (b. 1948)*

Alternative tune: WOODLANDS, no. 29

Go forth and tell! O Church of God, awake!
God's saving news to all the nations take:
proclaim Christ Jesus, Saviour, Lord, and King,
that all the world his worthy praise may sing.

2   Go forth and tell! God's love embraces all;
he will in grace respond to all who call:
how shall they call if they have never heard
the gracious invitation of his word?

3   Go forth and tell! Where still the darkness lies
in wealth or want, the sinner surely dies:
give us, O Lord, concern of heart and mind,
a love like yours which cares for humankind.

4   Go forth and tell! The doors are open wide:
share God's good gifts—let no one be denied;
live out your life as Christ your Lord shall choose,
your ransomed powers for his sole glory use.

5   Go forth and tell! O Church of God, arise!
Go in the strength which Christ your Lord supplies;
go till all nations his great name adore
and serve him, Lord and King for evermore.

James Seddon (1915–83)

81 God has spoken

God has spoken

Israeli traditional melody
arr. Norman Warren (b. 1934)
Descant by Angela Reith (b. 1952)

God has spo - ken to his peo - ple, al - le - lu - ia,

and his words are words of wis - dom, al - le - lu - ia!

1. O - pen your ears, O Christ-ian peo - ple, o - pen your ears and
2. They who have ears to hear his mes-sage, they who have ears, then
3. Is - ra - el comes to greet the sa - viour, Ju - dah is glad to

GLORY TO GOD IN THE CHURCH

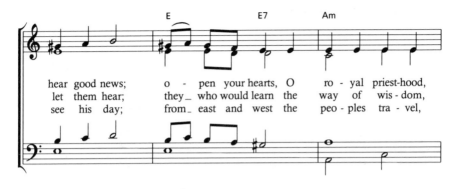

God has spoken to his people, alleluia,
and his words are words of wisdom, alleluia!

Open your ears, O Christian people,
open your ears and hear good news;
open your hearts, O royal priesthood,
God has come to you, God has come to you.

2   They who have ears to hear his message,
they who have ears, then let them hear;
they who would learn the way of wisdom,
let them hear God's word, let them hear God's word.

3   Israel comes to greet the saviour,
Judah is glad to see his day;
from east and west the peoples travel,
he will show the way, he will show the way.

Willard Jabusch (b. 1930)

169

82 God is here!

Ivinghoe   87 87 D   *Greville Cooke (1894–1989)*

Alternative tunes: LUX EOI, no. 75; ABBOT'S LEIGH, no. 10

God is here! As we his people
meet to offer praise and prayer,
may we find in fuller measure
what it is in Christ we share.
Here, as in the world around us,
all our varied skills and arts
wait the coming of his Spirit
into open minds and hearts.

2   Here are symbols to remind us
of our lifelong need of grace;
here are table, font and pulpit;
here the cross has central place.
Here in honesty of preaching,
here in silence as in speech,
here, in newness and renewal,
God the Spirit comes to each.

3   Here our children find a welcome
in the Shepherd's flock and fold.
Here, as bread and wine are taken,
Christ sustains us as of old.
Here the servants of the Servant
seek in worship to explore
what it means in daily living
to believe and to adore.

4   Lord of all, of Church and kingdom,
in an age of change and doubt,
keep us faithful to the Gospel,
help us work your purpose out.
Here, in this day's dedication,
all we have to give, receive:
we, who cannot live without you,
we adore you! We believe!

Fred Pratt Green (b. 1903)

83 How firm a foundation

Roxburgh   11 11 11 11

Henry Smart (1813–79)

How firm a foundation, you people of God,
is laid for your faith in his excellent word!
What more can he say to you than he has said
to everyone trusting in Jesus, our head?

2 Since Jesus is with you, do not be afraid;
since he is your Lord, you need not be dismayed:
he strengthens you, guards you, and helps you to stand,
upheld by his righteous, omnipotent hand.

3 When through the deep waters he calls you to go,
the rivers of trouble shall not overflow;
the Lord will be with you, to help and to bless,
and work for your good through your deepest distress.

4 When through fiery trials your pathway shall lead,
his grace shall sustain you with all that you need;
the flames shall not hurt you—his only design
your dross to consume and your gold to refine.

5 Whoever has come to believe in his name
will not be deserted, and not put to shame;
though hell may endeavour that Christian to shake,
his Lord will not leave him, nor ever forsake.

Richard Keen (c.1787)
and in this version Jubilate Hymns

84 Humbly in your sight

Humbly in your sight   11 11

Traditional North Malawian melody
adpt. Tom Colvin (b. 1925)
arr. John Bell (b. 1949)

This song is best sung unaccompanied.

Humbly in your sight we come together, Lord,
grant us now the blessing of your presence here.

2 These, our hearts, are yours, we give them to you, Lord,
purify our love to make it like your own.

3 These, our eyes, are yours, we give them to you, Lord,
may we always see your world as with your sight.

4 These, our hands, are yours, we give them to you, Lord,
give them strength and skill to do all work for you.

5 These, our feet, are yours, we give them to you, Lord,
may we always walk the path of life with you.

6 These, our tongues, are yours, we give them to you, Lord,
may we speak your healing words of life and truth.

7 These, our ears, are yours, we give them to you, Lord,
open them to hear the Gospel as from you.

8 Our whole selves are yours, we give them to you, Lord,
take us now and keep us yours for evermore.

Tumbuka hymn by J. P. Chirwa
tr. and adpt. by Tom Colvin (b. 1925)

85 Jesus is risen from the grave

Childer   *John Bell (b. 1949)*

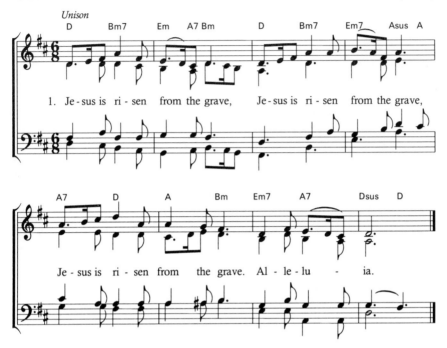

Jesus is risen from the grave,
Jesus is risen from the grave,
Jesus is risen from the grave.
Alleluia.

2   Jesus was seen by Mary . . .

3   Peter will soon be smiling . . .

4   Thomas will stop his doubting . . .

5   Jesus will meet his people . . .

6   Jesus is here with bread and wine . . .

7   Jesus will live for ever . . .

John Bell (b. 1949)
Graham Maule (b. 1958)

Words & music © The Iona Community/Wild Goose Publications.

86 Christ making friends

FIRST TUNE

Dove of peace   86 86 (CM) extended

American traditional melody
arr. Austin C. Lovelace (b. 1919)

I come with joy to meet my Lord,
forgiven, loved, and free,
in awe and wonder to recall
his life laid down for me.

2   I come with Christians far and near
to find, as all are fed,
the new community of love
in Christ's communion bread.

3 As Christ breaks bread and bids us share
each proud division ends.
The love that made us, makes us one,
and strangers now are friends.

4 And thus with joy we meet our Lord,
his presence, always near,
is in such friendship better known:
we see, and praise him here.

5 Together met, together bound,
we'll go our different ways,
and as his people in the world
we'll live and speak his praise.

Brian Wren (b. 1936)

Repeat the last line of each verse when using the first tune, DOVE OF PEACE.

Words © B. A. Wren/Oxford University Press.

SECOND TUNE

St Botolph   86 86 (CM)   *Gordon Slater (1896–1979)*

87 Jesus went to worship

Camber   65 65

Martin Shaw (1875–1958)

Jesus went to worship
in the synagogue;
with his friends and neighbours
sang his praise to God.

2 We, like Jesus, worship
in the Church today;
still, with friends and neighbours,
sing our songs and pray.

3 When the service ended
Jesus took his praise
into streets and houses
spelling out God's ways.

4 People came to Jesus,
frightened, hurt and sad;
helping them to worship,
Jesus made them glad.

5 Holy Spirit, help us
when this service ends,
still to follow Jesus,
still to be his friends.

6 When our neighbours meet us,
may they, with surprise,
catch a glimpse of Jesus
rising in our eyes.

Alan Gaunt (b. 1935)

88 Lord, where have we left you?

The Lichtbob's Lassie 65 76

Scottish traditional melody
arr. John Bell (b. 1949)

1. Lord, where have we left you— some-where far a - way, re - mote and in the

Verse 5

man-ger, a stran-ger, still in hay?_ Lord, you ne - ver leave us.

Lord, where have we left you—
somewhere far away,
remote and in the manger,
a stranger, still in hay?

2 Lord, where have we left you—
somewhere lost to light,
submerged in doubt or dreaming
and seeming out of sight?

3 Lord, where have we left you—
somewhere all can view,
well-polished and presented,
undented and untrue?

4 Lord, where have we left you—
somewhere out of range,
divorced from thoughts that matter,
that shatter, cheat or change?

5 Lord, you never leave us,
though you're left behind.
To where you call and need us,
now lead us and our kind.

Lord, you never leave us.

John Bell (b. 1949)
Graham Maule (b. 1958)

89 Lord of the Church

Londonderry air   11 10 11 10 D

Irish traditional melody
arr. John Barnard (b. 1948)

Words © T. Dudley-Smith. Arrangement © J. Barnard/Jubilate Hymns.

Lord of the Church, we pray for our renewing:
Christ over all, our undivided aim.
Fire of the Spirit, burn for our enduing,
wind of the Spirit, fan the living flame!
We turn to Christ amid our fear and failing,
the will that lacks the courage to be free,
the weary labours, all but unavailing,
to bring us nearer what a Church should be.

2 Lord of the Church, we seek a Father's blessing,
a true repentance and a faith restored,
a swift obedience and a new possessing,
filled with the Holy Spirit of the Lord!
We turn to Christ from all our restless striving,
unnumbered voices with a single prayer—
the living water from our souls' reviving,
in Christ to live, and love and serve and care.

3 Lord of the Church, we long for our uniting,
true to one calling, by one vision stirred;
one cross proclaiming and one creed reciting,
one in the truth of Jesus and his word!
So lead us on; till toil and trouble ended,
one Church triumphant one new song shall sing,
to praise his glory, risen and ascended,
Christ over all, the everlasting King!

Timothy Dudley-Smith (b. 1926)

90 Love is his word

Cresswell   88 97 with refrain

Anthony Milner (b. 1925)
Refrain harm. Helen Killick (b. 1965)

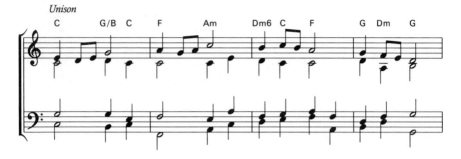

Rich - er than gold is the love of my Lord:_ bet - ter than splen-dour or wealth.

Love is his word, love is his way,
feasting with men, fasting alone,
living and dying, rising again,
love, only love, is his way.

Richer than gold is the love of my Lord:
better than splendour or wealth.

2 Love is his way, love is his mark,
sharing his last Passover feast,
Christ at his table, host to the twelve,
love, only love, is his mark.

3 Love is his mark, love is his sign,
bread for our strength, wine for our joy,
'This is my body, this is my blood.'
Love, only love, is his sign.

4 Love is his sign, love is his news;
'Do this,' he said, 'lest you forget
all my deep sorrow, all my dear blood.'
Love, only love, is his news.

5 Love is his news, love is his name,
we are his own, chosen and called,
family, brethren, cousins and kin.
Love, only love, is his name.

6 Love is his name, love is his law;
hear his command, all who are his:
'Love one another, I have loved you.'
Love, only love, is his law.

7 Love is his law, love is his word:
love of the Lord, Father and Word,
love of the Spirit, God ever one.
Love, only love, is his word.

Luke Connaughton (1917–79)

91 Make way, for Christ the King

Make way

Graham Kendrick (b. 1950)
arr. Paul Bateman (b. 1954)

1. Make way, make way, for Christ the King in splen - dour ar - rives. Fling wide the gates and wel - come him in - to your lives. Make way! Make way for the King of kings! Make way for the King of kings! Make

Make way, make way, for Christ the King
in splendour arrives.
Fling wide the gates and welcome him
into your lives.

Make way! Make way
for the King of kings!
Make way! Make way
and let his kingdom in.

2 He comes the broken hearts to heal,
the prisoners to free;
the deaf shall hear, the lame shall dance,
the blind shall see.

3 And those who mourn with heavy hearts,
who weep and sigh,
with laughter, joy and royal crown
he'll beautify.

4 We call you now to worship him
as Lord of all,
to have no other gods but him;
their thrones must fall.

Graham Kendrick (b. 1950)

92 May the Lord, mighty God

Wen ti

Chinese melody
adpt. I-to Loh (b. 1936)

1. May the Lord, might-y God, bless and keep you for e - ver;

grant you peace, per-fect peace, cou-rage in ev-'ry en - dea - vour.

DESCANT

2. Lift up and see his face, his

MELODY

2. Lift up your eyes and see his face, and his

grace for e - ver; may the Lord,

grace for e - ver; may the Lord,

might - y God, bless and keep you for e - ver.

might - y God, bless and keep you for e - ver.

This song is best sung unaccompanied.

Traditional blessing

93 Night has fallen

God our maker

Traditional Malawian evening hymn
arr. John Bell (b. 1949)

(*Cantor*) 4   You have kept us, Lord.
(*All*)   You have kept us, Lord.
God our maker,
guard us sleeping.

5   See your children, Lord.   6   Keep us in your love.   7   Now we go to rest.

Chewa hymn
tr. Tom Colvin (b. 1925)

This song is best sung unaccompanied.

94 Now let us from this table rise

Killibegs   88 88 (LM)   *William Davies (b. 1921)*

1. Now let us from this ta - ble rise_____ re-newed in

bo - dy, mind and soul;_____ with Christ we die and live a -

- gain,_____ his self - less love has made us whole.

Now let us from this table rise
renewed in body, mind and soul;
with Christ we die and live again,
his selfless love has made us whole.

2   With minds alert, upheld by grace,
to spread the Word in speech and deed,
we follow in the steps of Christ,
at one with all in hope and need.

3   To fill each human house with love,
it is the sacrament of care;
the work that Christ began to do
we humbly pledge ourselves to share.

4   Then give us courage, Father-God,
to choose again the pilgrim way,
and help us to accept with joy
the challenge of tomorrow's day.

Fred Kaan (b. 1929)

95 Powerful in making us wise

FIRST TUNE

Liebster Immanuel   11 10 11 10

*Melody from 'Himmels-Lust' (1679)
harm. J. S. Bach (1685–1750)*

GLORY TO GOD IN THE CHURCH

SECOND TUNE

Yvonne   11 10 11 10

Norman Warren (b. 1934)

Music © N. Warren/Jubilate Hymns.

Powerful in making us wise to salvation,
witness to faith in Christ Jesus the Word;
breathed out for all by the life-giving Father—
these are the scriptures, and thus speaks the Lord.

2   Tool for employment and compass for travel,
map in the desert and lamp in the dark;
teaching, rebuking, correcting and training—
these are the scriptures, and this is their work.

3   History, prophecy, song and commandment,
gospel and letter and dream from on high;
written by those borne along by the Spirit—
these are the scriptures; on them we rely.

4   Gift for God's servants to fit them completely,
fully equipping to walk in his ways;
guide to good work and effective believing—
these are the scriptures, for these we give praise!

Christopher Idle (b. 1938)

96 Praise the Lord in everything!

Praise the Lord   11 10 11 9

Leslie Osborne

1. Praise the Lord in the rhy-thm of your mu-sic, praise the Lord in the free-dom of your dance, praise the Lord in the coun-try and the ci-ty, praise him in the li-ving of your life!   earth!

Praise the Lord in the rhythm of your music,
praise the Lord in the freedom of your dance,
praise the Lord in the country and the city,
praise him in the living of your life!

2 Praise the Lord on the organ and piano,
praise the Lord on guitar and on the drums,
praise the Lord on the tambourine and cymbals,
praise him in the singing of your song!

3 Praise the Lord with the movement of your bodies,
praise the Lord with the clapping of your hands,
praise the Lord with your poetry and painting,
praise him in the acting of your play!

4 Praise the Lord in the feeding of the hungry,
praise the Lord in the healing of disease,
praise the Lord as you show his love in action,
praise him in your caring for the poor!

5 Praise the Lord, every nation, every people,
praise the Lord, men and women, old and young,
praise the Lord, let us celebrate together,
praise him everything in heaven and earth!

Peter Casey

97 Shout for joy

Lansdowne   99 99

John Bell (b. 1949)

1. Shout for joy! The ___ Lord has let us feast; ___
heav'n's own fare has ___ fed the last and least; ___
Christ's own peace is shared a-gain ___ on earth; ___
Christ's own peace is shared a-gain, *is shared on earth;* ___
(3.) voi-ces, *voi-ces ring:* ___
God the Spi-rit ___ fills us with new worth.

Words & music © 1989 The Iona Community/Wild Goose Publications.

Shout for joy! The Lord has let us feast;
heaven's own fare has fed the last and least;
Christ's own peace *is shared* again *on earth;*
God the Spirit fills us with new worth.

2   No more doubting, no more senseless dread:
God's good self has graced our wine and bread;
all the wonder heaven *has kept in store*
now is ours to keep for evermore.

3   Celebrate with saints who dine on high,
witnesses that love can never die.
'Hallelujah!'—thus their *voices ring:*
nothing less in gratitude we bring.

4   Praise the Maker, praise the Maker's Son,
praise the Spirit—three yet ever one;
praise the God *whose* food and *friends avow*
heaven starts here! The kingdom beckons now!

John Bell (b. 1949)
Graham Maule (b. 1958)

In the third line of each verse, basses repeat the italicized words.

98 Spirit of God

Skye Boat Song 86 86 (CM) with refrain

Scottish traditional melody
arr. Donald Davison (b. 1937)

REFRAIN

Spi - rit of God, un - seen as the wind, gen - tle as is the dove; teach us the truth and help us be - lieve, show us the Sa - viour's love.

VERSE

1. You spoke to us long, long a - go,

Spirit of God, unseen as the wind,
gentle as is the dove;
teach us the truth and help us believe,
show us the Saviour's love.

1 You spoke to us long, long ago,
   gave us the written word;
   we read it still, needing its truth,
   through it God's voice is heard.

2 Without your help we fail our Lord,
   we cannot live his way;
   we need your power, we need your strength,
   following Christ each day.

Margaret Old (b. 1932)

99 Thanks to God

St Helen   87 87 87   *George Martin (1844–1916)*

Small notes are for organ only.

Thanks to God whose word was spoken
in the deed that made the earth.
His the voice that called a nation,
his the fires that tried her worth.
God has spoken, God has spoken:
praise him for his open word.

2   Thanks to God whose word incarnate
glorified the flesh of man.
Deeds and words and death and rising
tell the grace in heaven's plan.
God has spoken, God has spoken:
praise him for his open word.

3   Thanks to God whose word was written
in the Bible's sacred page,
record of the revelation
showing God to every age.
God has spoken, God has spoken:
praise him for his open word.

4   Thanks to God whose word is published
in the tongues of every race.
See its glory undiminished
by the change of time or place.
God has spoken, God has spoken:
praise him for his open word.

5   Thanks to God whose word is answered
by the Spirit's voice within.
Here we drink of joy unmeasured,
life redeemed from death and sin.
God is speaking, God is speaking:
praise him for his open word.

R. T. Brooks (1918–85)

100 To him we come

Living Lord   98 88 83

Patrick Appleford (b. 1925)

1. To him we come—
Jesus Christ our Lord,
God's own living Word, his dear Son:
in him there is no east and west,
in him all nations shall be blessed;
to all he offers peace and rest—
loving

Lord!   Lord!

To him we come—
Jesus Christ our Lord,
God's own living Word,
his dear Son:
in him there is no east and west,
in him all nations shall be blessed;
to all he offers peace and rest—
loving Lord!

2 In him we live—
Christ our strength and stay,
life and truth and way,
friend divine:
his power can break the chains of sin,
still all life's storms without, within,
help us the daily fight to win—
living Lord!

3 For him we go—
soldiers of the cross,
counting all things loss
him to know;
going to every land and race,
preaching to all redeeming grace,
building his Church in every place—
conquering Lord!

4 With him we serve—
his the work we share
with saints everywhere,
near and far;
one in the task which faith requires,
one in the zeal which never tires,
one in the hope his love inspires—
coming Lord!

5 Onward we go—
faithful, bold, and true,
called his will to do
day by day,
till, at the last, with joy we'll see
Jesus, in glorious majesty;
live with him through eternity—
reigning Lord!

James Seddon (1915–83)

(harmony version overleaf)

Harmony

1. To him we come— Je - sus Christ our Lord, God's own li - ving Word, his dear Son: in him there is no east and west, in him all na - tions shall be blessed; to all he of - fers peace and rest— lo - ving

To him we come—
Jesus Christ our Lord,
God's own living Word,
his dear Son:
in him there is no east and west,
in him all nations shall be blessed;
to all he offers peace and rest—
loving Lord!

2 In him we live—
Christ our strength and stay,
life and truth and way,
friend divine:
his power can break the chains of sin,
still all life's storms without, within,
help us the daily fight to win—
living Lord!

3 For him we go—
soldiers of the cross,
counting all things loss
him to know;
going to every land and race,
preaching to all redeeming grace,
building his Church in every place—
conquering Lord!

4 With him we serve—
his the work we share
with saints everywhere,
near and far;
one in the task which faith requires,
one in the zeal which never tires,
one in the hope his love inspires—
coming Lord!

5 Onward we go—
faithful, bold, and true,
called his will to do
day by day,
till, at the last, with joy we'll see
Jesus, in glorious majesty;
live with him through eternity—
reigning Lord!

James Seddon (1915–83)

101 We are marching in the light of God

Siyahamba

South African traditional melody
arr. Anders Nyberg and compilers of 'Rejoice and Sing'

1. We are march - ing in the light of God, we are
   Si - ya - hamb' _____ e - ku - kha - nyen' kwen - khos', Si - ya -

march-ing in the light of God.
- hamb' e - ku - kha - nyen' kwen - khos'.

1 | 2
God.
- khos'.

the light of God.
kha - nyen' kwen - khos'.

God.
- khos'.

We are march - ing, _____ oh, _____ we are
Si - ya - ham - ba, _____ oo, _____ si - ya -

We are march-ing, march-ing, we are march-ing, march-ing, we are
Si - ya - ham - ba, ham - ba, si - ya - ham - ba, ham - ba, si - ya -

We are marching in the light of God,
we are marching in the light of God. } *twice*

We are marching, oh,
we are marching in the light of God. } *twice*

2   We are living in the love of God. (*etc.*)

3   We are moving in the power of God. (*etc.*)

South African traditional
tr. Anders Nyberg, 1984

Original text: *Siyahamb' ekukhanyen' kwenkhos'.*

102 We believe in God Almighty

Corde natus   87 87 87 7

Melody from 'Piae Cantiones', 1582
arr. David Iliff (b. 1939)

We believe in God Almighty,
maker of the earth and sky;
all we see and all that's hidden
is his work unceasingly:
God our Father's loving kindness
with us till the day we die—
evermore and evermore.

2   We believe in Christ the Saviour,
Son of God and Son of Man;
born of Mary, preaching, healing,
crucified, yet risen again:
he ascended to the Father
there in glory long to reign—
evermore and evermore.

3   We believe in God the Spirit,
present in our lives today;
speaking through the prophets' writings,
guiding travellers on their way:
to our hearts he brings forgiveness
and the hope of endless joy—
evermore and evermore.

David Mowbray (b. 1938)

207

103 We cannot measure how you heal

Ye banks and braes   88 88 D (DLM)

Scottish traditional melody
arr. John Bell (b. 1949)

An alternative arrangement of this tune (in F) may be found at no. 24.

GLORY TO GOD IN THE CHURCH

hold _ and heal _ and _ warn, _ to _ car - ry all _ through

death to life _ and cra - dle _ child - ren yet _ un - born.

We cannot measure how you heal
or answer every sufferer's prayer,
yet we believe your grace responds
where faith and doubt unite to care.
Your hands, though bloodied on the cross,
survive to hold and heal and warn,
to carry all through death to life
and cradle children yet unborn.

2 The pain that will not go away,
the guilt that clings from things long past,
the fear of what the future holds,
are present as if meant to last.
But present too is love which tends
the hurt we never hoped to find,
the private agonies inside,
the memories that haunt the mind.

3 So some have come who need your help
and some have come to make amends,
as hands which shaped and saved the world
are present in the touch of friends.
Lord, let your Spirit meet us here
to mend the body, mind and soul,
to disentangle peace from pain
and make your broken people whole.

John Bell (b. 1949)
Graham Maule (b. 1958)

104 We come as guests invited

FIRST TUNE

Passion Chorale   76 76 D

Hans Leo Hassler (1564–1612)
harm. J. S. Bach (1685–1750)

We come as guests invited
when Jesus bids us dine,
his friends on earth united
to share the bread and wine;
the bread of life is broken,
the wine is freely poured
for us, in solemn token
of Christ our dying Lord.

2   We eat and drink, receiving
from Christ the grace we need,
and in our hearts believing
on him by faith we feed;
with wonder and thanksgiving
for love that knows no end,
we find in Jesus living
our ever-present friend.

3   One bread is ours for sharing,
one single fruitful vine,
our fellowship declaring
renewed in bread and wine—
renewed, sustained and given
by token, sign and word,
the pledge and seal of heaven,
the love of Christ our Lord.

Timothy Dudley-Smith (b. 1926)

(104) We come as guests invited
SECOND TUNE

Salley Gardens   76 76 D

Irish traditional melody
arr. Oxford University Press

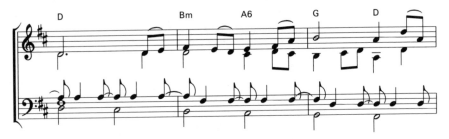

Arrangement © Oxford University Press.

GLORY TO GOD IN THE CHURCH

We come as guests invited
when Jesus bids us dine,
his friends on earth united
to share the bread and wine;
the bread of life is broken,
the wine is freely poured
for us, in solemn token
of Christ our dying Lord.

2 We eat and drink, receiving
from Christ the grace we need,
and in our hearts believing
on him by faith we feed;
with wonder and thanksgiving
for love that knows no end,
we find in Jesus living
our ever-present friend.

3 One bread is ours for sharing,
one single fruitful vine,
our fellowship declaring
renewed in bread and wine—
renewed, sustained and given
by token, sign and word,
the pledge and seal of heaven,
the love of Christ our Lord.

Timothy Dudley-Smith (b. 1926)

105 We gather here his friends to meet

Gaelic lullaby 88 87

*Scottish tradtional melody
arr. Helen Killick (b. 1965)*

1. We ga - ther here ___ his friends ___ to meet, his

friends ___ to meet, his friends to meet. We ga - ther here ___ his

friends to meet, the friends of our ___ Lord Je - sus.

We gather here his friends to meet,
his friends to meet, his friends to meet.
We gather here his friends to meet,
the friends of our Lord Jesus.

2   We gather here our lives to mend,
our lives to mend, our lives to mend.
We gather here our lives to mend,
to offer them to Jesus.

3   We gather here the world to heal . . .
We gather here the world to heal,
the world so loved by Jesus.

4   We gather here his bread to break . . .
We gather here his bread to break,
the body of Lord Jesus.

5   We promise here his truth to live . . .
We promise here his truth to live,
the truth of our Lord Jesus.

6   We go from here his way to seek . . .
We go from here his way to seek,
to follow our Lord Jesus.

Anna Briggs (b. 1947)

106 We have a gospel

Fulda (Walton)   88 88 (LM)

Gardiner's 'Sacred Melodies', 1815

We have a gospel to proclaim,
good news for all throughout the earth;
the gospel of a Saviour's name:
we sing his glory, tell his worth.

2 Tell of his birth at Bethlehem,
not in a royal house or hall
but in a stable dark and dim,
the Word made flesh, a light for all.

3 Tell of his death at Calvary,
hated by those he came to save,
in lonely suffering on the cross;
for all he loved his life he gave.

4 Tell of that glorious Easter morn:
empty the tomb, for he was free.
He broke the power of death and hell
that we might share his victory.

5 Tell of his reign at God's right hand,
by all creation glorified.
He sends his Spirit on his Church
to live for him, the Lamb who died.

6 Now we rejoice to name him King:
Jesus is Lord of all the earth.
This Gospel-message we proclaim:
we sing his glory, tell his worth.

Edward Burns (b. 1938)

107 Rejoice!

Rejoice

Graham Kendrick (b. 1950)

GLORY TO GOD IN THE CHURCH

VERSE

A   Bm

1. Now is the time for us to march up-on the land, in-to our
2. God is at work in us his pur-pose to per-form, build-ing a
3. Though we are weak, his grace is ev-'ry-thing we need; we're made of

G   A   D

hands he will give the ground we claim._____
king - dom of po - wer not of words,_____
clay but this trea-sure is with - in._____

A   Bm

He rides in ma - jes - ty to lead us in - to vic - to-ry,
where things im - pos - si - ble by faith shall be made pos - si - ble;
He turns our weak-ness-es in - to his op - por - tu - ni-ties,

G   Bm   Em7   Asus   A   *D.C.*

the world shall see that Christ is Lord!_____
let's give the glo - ry to him now._____ *Re -*
so that the glo - ry goes to him._____

219

108 All the ends of the earth

All the ends of the earth

Words and music by Bob Dufford
Words from Psalm 98
arr. Helen Killick (b. 1965)

GLORY TO GOD IN THE WORLD

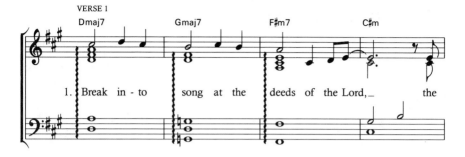

VERSE 1

Dmaj7   Gmaj7   F#m7   C#m

1. Break in - to song at the deeds of the Lord, _ the

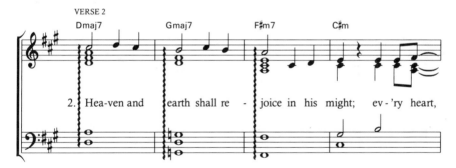

F#m   Bm7   Esus   REFRAIN E7 *D.C.*

won-ders he has done _ in ev - 'ry age. _

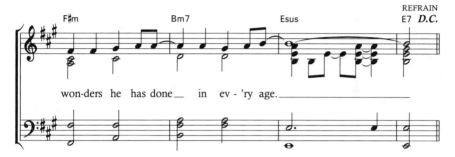

VERSE 2

Dmaj7   Gmaj7   F#m7   C#m

2. Hea-ven and earth shall re - joice in his might; ev - 'ry heart,

REFRAIN *& v.3 overleaf*

F#m   Bm7   Esus   E7

_ ev - 'ry na - tion call him Lord. _

GLORY TO GOD

REFRAIN

All the ends of the earth, __ all you crea-tures of the sea, __

lift up your eyes to the won - ders of the Lord; __ for the

Lord of the earth, __ the Mas - ter of the sea, __ has

come with jus - tice for the world. __

GLORY TO GOD IN THE WORLD

VERSE 3

3. The Lord has made his sal - va - tion known,

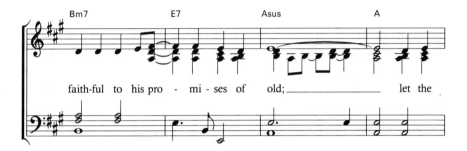

faith-ful to his pro - mi - ses of old;_____ let the

ends of the earth,_ let the sea and all it__ holds make

Repeat REFRAIN *al Fine*

mu - sic be - fore our King!_____

109 Lights to the world

Lights to the world

John Daniels
and Phil Thomson
arr. Christopher Norton

1. All earth was dark un - til you spoke— then all was light and all was peace; yet still, O God, so ma - ny — wait to see the flame of love re - leased.

REFRAIN

Lights to the world! O Light di - vine, kin - dle in us a

might-y_ flame,   till ev-'ry heart, con-sumed by love, shall   rise   to__

praise your ho - ly name!

All earth was dark until you spoke—
then all was light and all was peace;
yet still, O God, so many wait
to see the flame of love released.

Lights to the world! O Light divine,
kindle in us a mighty flame,
till every heart, consumed by love,
shall rise to praise your holy name!

2   In Christ you gave your gift of life
    to save us from the depth of night:
    O come and set our spirits free
    and draw us to your perfect light!

3   Where there is fear may we bring joy,
    and healing to a world in pain:
    Lord, build your kingdom through our lives
    till Jesus walks this earth again.

4   O burn in us, that we may burn
    with love that triumphs in despair;
    and touch our lives with such a fire
    that souls may search and find you there.

John Daniels and Phil Thomson

110 For the fruits of his creation

East Acklam   84 84 88 84   *Francis Jackson (b. 1917)*

Alternative tune: AR HYD Y NOS, no. 76

For the fruits of his creation,
thanks be to God;
for his gifts to every nation,
thanks be to God;
for the ploughing, sowing, reaping,
silent growth while we are sleeping,
future needs in earth's safe-keeping,
thanks be to God.

2 In the just reward of labour,
God's will is done;
in the help we give our neighbour,
God's will is done;
in our worldwide task of caring
for the hungry and despairing,
in the harvests we are sharing,
God's will is done.

3 For the harvests of his Spirit,
thanks be to God;
for the good we all inherit,
thanks be to God;
for the wonders that astound us,
for the truths that still confound us,
most of all that love has found us,
thanks be to God.

Fred Pratt Green (b. 1903)

111 For the healing of the nations

St Columbanus   87 87 87

Walter Newport (1839–?)
harm. Henry Rosevear (b. 1903)

For the healing of the nations,
Lord, we pray with one accord;
for a just and equal sharing
of the things that earth affords.
To a life of love in action
help us rise and pledge our word.

2   Lead us, Father, into freedom,
from despair your world release;
that, redeemed from war and hatred,
all may come and go in peace.
Show us how through care and goodness
fear will die and hope increase.

3   All that kills abundant living,
let it from the earth be banned;
pride of status, race or schooling,
dogmas that obscure your plan.
In our common quest for justice
may we hallow life's brief span.

4   You, creator-God, have written
your great name on humankind;
for our growing in your likeness
bring the life of Christ to mind;
that by our response and service
earth its destiny may find.

Fred Kaan (b. 1929)

112 For the world and all its people

Somos pueblo que camina   87 87

Nicaraguan melody
arr. Iona Community

For the world and all its people,
we address our prayers to God.

Confidently, all can worship
in the presence of the Lord.

2 All the powerless, all the hungry
are most precious to their God.

3 For the poor, God has a purpose,
for the desperate, a word.

4 Christ is here, and Christ is stronger
than the strength of sin or sword.

5 God will fill the earth with justice
when our will and his accord.

from the Misa Popular Nicaraguense
adpt. and tr. Iona Community

113 God in his love for us

Stewardship   11 10 11 10

Valerie Ruddle (b. 1932)

God in his love for us lent us this planet,
gave it a purpose in time and in space:
small as a spark from the fire of creation,
cradle of life and the home of our race.

2   Thanks be to God for its bounty and beauty,
life that sustains us in body and mind:
plenty for all, if we learn how to share it,
riches undreamed of to fathom and find.

3   Long have our human wars ruined its harvest;
long has earth bowed to the terror of force;
long have we wasted what others have need of,
poisoned the fountain of life at its source.

4   Earth is the Lord's: it is ours to enjoy it,
ours, as his stewards, to farm and defend.
From its pollution, misuse and destruction,
good Lord, deliver us, world without end!

Fred Pratt Green (b. 1903)

114 From the darkness came light

From the darkness

Jancis Harvey (b. 1944)

REFRAIN
INSTRUMENTAL DESCANT

Unison

From the dark-ness came light, from the black-est of nights;

wait for the morn-ing, the sun-light, the dawn-ing; from the dark-ness came light.

VERSES 1 & 2

1. Earth so dark and so cold, what great se - crets you
2. Je - sus born in a stall, born to bring light to

GLORY TO GOD IN THE WORLD

hold; / all.
the pro-mise of spring, the
He came to love us,___ new

won-der you bring, the beau-ty of na-ture un-folds.
life to give us;___ Je-sus was born_ in a stall.

VERSE 3

3. Je-sus died_ on Cal-v'ry, suff-'red for you_ and for me; he

rose from the dark and gloom, out of a sto-ny tomb, walked in the world and was free.

VERSE 4

4. We have this new_ life to share, a love to pass on__ ev-'ry-where;

time spent in gi-ving, a joy in our li-ving, in show-ing to o-thers we care.

115 Jesu, Jesu

Chereponi   779 with refrain

Traditional Ghanaian melody
adpt. Tom Colvin (b. 1925)
arr. Oxford University Press

1. Kneels at the feet of his friends, si-lent-ly wash-es their

1. Kneels at the feet of his friends,_____

feet; mas-ter who acts as a slave_____ to them._

si-lent-ly wash-es their feet;_____ *acts as a slave to them._*

REFRAIN

Je - su,_____ Je - su,_____ fill

This song is best sung unaccompanied.

us with your love, show us how to serve the neigh-bours we have from you.

Kneels at the feet of his friends,
silently washes their feet;
master who *acts as a slave to them.*

Jesu, Jesu, fill us with your love,
show us how to serve
the neighbours we have from you.

2   Neighbours are both rich and poor,
neighbours are black, brown and white,
neighbours are *nearby and far away.*

3   These are the ones we should serve,
these are the ones we should love,
all these are *neighbours to us and you.*

4   Loving puts us on our knees,
serving as though we are slaves,
this is the way we should live with you.

Tom Colvin (b. 1925)

'Jesu' should be pronounced 'Yay-soo'. In the third line of each verse, tenors and basses sing the italicized words.

116 Lord, for the years

Lord of the years 11 10 11 10

Michael Baughen (b. 1930)
arr. David Iliff (b. 1939)

Small notes are for the accompaniment only.

Lord, for the years your love has kept and guided,
urged and inspired us, cheered us on our way,
sought us and saved us, pardoned and provided:
Lord of the years, we bring our thanks today.

2 Lord, for that word, the word of life which fires us,
speaks to our hearts and sets our souls ablaze,
teaches and trains, rebukes us and inspires us:
Lord of the word, receive your people's praise.

3 Lord, for our land in this our generation,
spirits oppressed by pleasure, wealth and care:
for young and old, for this and every nation,
Lord of our land, be pleased to hear our prayer.

4 Lord, for our world; when we disown and doubt him,
loveless in strength, and comfortless in pain,
hungry and helpless, lost indeed without him:
Lord of the world, we pray that Christ may reign.

5 Lord for ourselves; in living power remake us—
self on the cross and Christ upon the throne,
past put behind us, for the future take us:
Lord of our lives, to live for Christ alone.

Timothy Dudley-Smith (b. 1926)

117 Lord, bring the day to pass

Little Cornard   66 66 88

Martin Shaw (1875–1958)

Small notes are for the accompaniment only.
Alternative tune: LOVE UNKNOWN, *Church Hymnary: Third Edition* no. 95,
Revised Church Hymnary no. 76

Lord, bring the day to pass
when forest, rock and hill,
the beasts, the birds, the grass,
will know your finished will:
when we attain our destiny
and nature its lost unity.

2 Forgive our careless use
of water, ore and soil—
the plenty we abuse
supplied by others' toil:
save us from making self our creed,
turn us towards each other's need.

3 Give us, when we release
creation's secret powers,
to harness them for peace,
our children's peace and ours:
teach us the art of mastering
which makes life rich and draws death's sting.

4 Creation groans, travails,
futile its present plight,
bound—till the hour it hails
God's children born of light
who enter on their true estate.
Come, Lord: new heavens and earth create.

Ian Fraser (b. 1917)

118 Shine, Jesus, shine

Shine, Jesus, shine

Words and music by
Graham Kendrick (b. 1950)

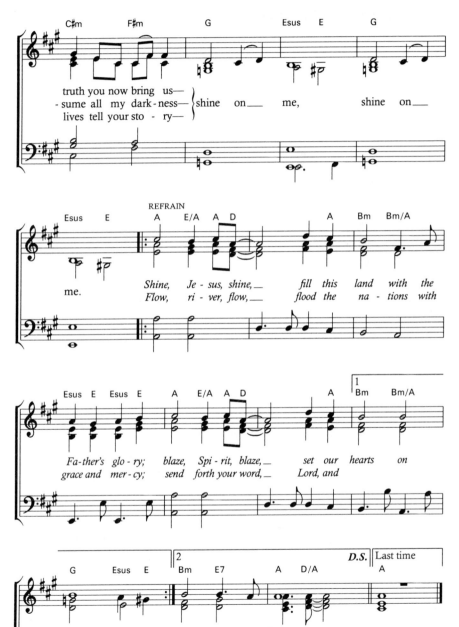

119 Lord, thy Church on earth is seeking

Everton 87 87 D *Henry Smart (1813–79)*

Alternative tune: ODE TO JOY, no. 28

Words © H. Sherlock

Lord, thy Church on earth is seeking
thy renewal from above;
teach us all the art of speaking
with the accent of thy love.
We will heed thy great commission:
Go ye into every place—
preach, baptize, fulfil my mission,
serve with love and share my grace.

2 Freedom give to those in bondage,
lift the burdens caused by sin.
Give new hope, new strength and courage,
grant release from fears within:
light for darkness; joy for sorrow;
love for hatred; peace for strife.
These and countless blessings follow
as the Spirit gives new life.

3 In the streets of every city
where the bruised and lonely dwell,
let us show the Saviour's pity,
let us of his mercy tell.
In all lands and with all races
let us serve, and seek to bring
all the world to render praises,
Christ, to thee, Redeemer, King.

Hugh Sherlock (b. 1905)

120 Morning has broken

Bunessan 55 54 D

Scottish traditional melody
arr. Donald Davison (b. 1937)

For an alternative arrangement see no. 38.

Morning has broken
like the first morning;
blackbird has spoken
like the first bird.
Praise for the singing!
Praise for the morning!
Praise for them, springing
fresh from the Word!

2 Sweet the rain's new fall
sunlit from heaven,
like the first dewfall
on the first grass.
Praise for the sweetness
of the wet garden,
sprung in completeness
where his feet pass.

3 Mine is the sunlight!
Mine is the morning
born of the one light
Eden saw play!
Praise with elation,
praise every morning,
God's re-creation
of the new day!

Eleanor Farjeon (1881–1965)

121 O Lord, all the world belongs to you

O Lord, all the world belongs to you

Patrick Appleford (b. 1925)

turn - ing   the   world   up   -   side   down.

O Lord, all the world belongs to you
and you are always making all things new.
What is wrong you forgive,
and the new life you give
is what's turning the world upside down.

2   The world's only loving to its friends,
but your way of loving never ends,
loving enemies too;
and this loving with you
is what's turning the world upside down.

3   The world lives divided and apart,
you draw us together, and we start
in our friendship to see
that in harmony we
can be turning the world upside down.

4   The world wants the wealth to live in state,
but you show a new way to be great:
like a servant you came,
and if we do the same,
we'll be turning the world upside down.

5   O Lord, all the world belongs to you
and you are always making all things new.
What is wrong you forgive,
and the new life you give
is what's turning the world upside down.

Patrick Appleford (b. 1925)

122   O Lord, the clouds are gathering

Gathering clouds

Words and music by
Graham Kendrick (b. 1950)

1. O__ Lord,__ the clouds are gath - er - ing, the fire of judge-ment
(2.) Lord,__ o - ver the na - tions now where is the dove of
(3.) Lord,__ dark pow'rs are poised to flood our streets with hate and
(4.) Lord,__ your glo - rious cross shall tower tri - umph - ant in this

burns,_____ how we have fal - len! O_____
peace?_____ Her wings are bro - ken. O_____
fear;_____ we must a - wa - ken! O_____
land,_____ e - vil con - found - ing. Through the

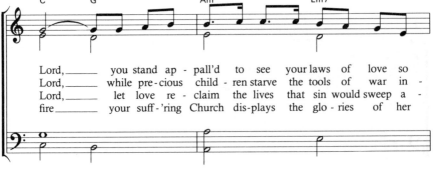

Lord,_____ you stand ap - pall'd to see your laws of love so
Lord,_____ while pre - cious child - ren starve the tools of war in -
Lord,_____ let love re - claim the lives that sin would sweep a -
fire_____ your suff - 'ring Church dis-plays the glo - ries of her

GLORY TO GOD IN THE WORLD

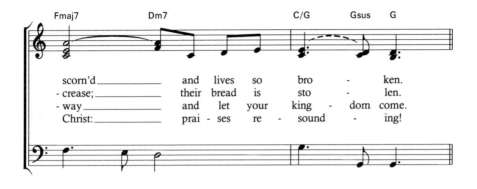

scorn'd_____ and lives so bro - ken.
- crease;_____ their bread is sto - len.
- way_____ and let your king - dom come.
Christ:_____ prai - ses re - sound - ing!

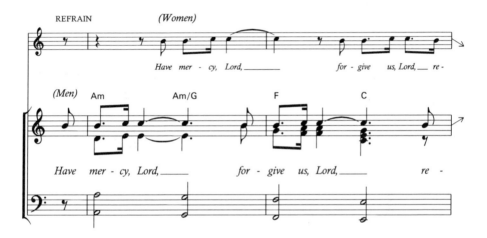

REFRAIN   (Women)

Have mer - cy, Lord,_____ for - give us, Lord,___ re -

(Men)   Am   Am/G   F   C

Have mer - cy, Lord,_____ for - give us, Lord,_____ re -

B   B7   Esus   E

- store us, Lord, re - vive your Church a - gain._____ Let

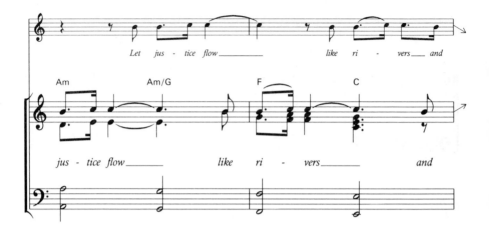

Let jus - tice flow _____ like ri - vers ___ and

jus - tice flow _____ like ri - vers _____ and

right - eous-ness like a ne - ver fail - ing stream.

2. O___ a ne-ver fail-ing stream. _____
3. O___
4. Yet, O

250

123 Out of our failure to create

Chorus Angelorum 86 86 (CM)   *Arthur Somervell (1863–1937)*

Out of our failure to create
a world of love and care;
out of the depths of human life
we cry to God in prayer.

2 Out of the darkness of our time,
of days for ever gone,
our souls are longing for the light,
like watchers for the dawn.

3 Out of the depths we cry to him
whose mercy ends our night.
Our human hole-and-corner ways
by him are brought to light.

4 Hope in the Lord whose timeless love
gives laughter where we wept;
the Father, who at every point
his word has given and kept.

Fred Kaan (b. 1929)

124 Restore, O Lord

Restore, O Lord

Words and music by Graham Kendrick (b. 1950)
and Chris Rolinson (b. 1958)
arr. David Peacock (b. 1949)

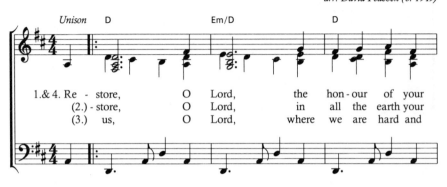

1.& 4. Re - store, O Lord, the hon - our of your
(2.) - store, O Lord, in all the earth your
(3.) us, O Lord, where we are hard and

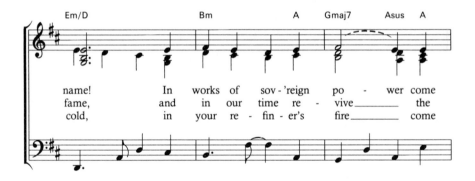

name! In works of sov - 'reign po - wer come
fame, and in our time re - vive the
cold, in your re - fin - er's fire come

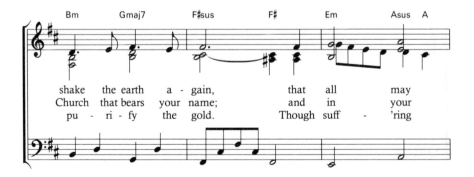

shake the earth a - gain, that all may
Church that bears your name; and in your
pu - ri - fy the gold. Though suff - 'ring

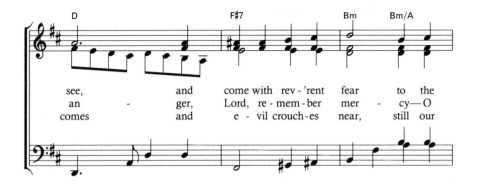

	and	come with rev - 'rent	fear	to the
	ger,	Lord, re - mem - ber	mer -	cy—O
	and	e - vil crouch - es	near,	still our

see,
an -
comes

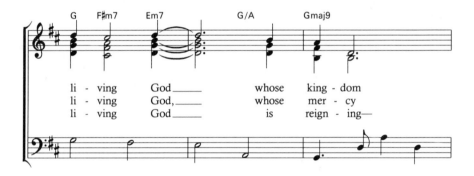

li - ving	God____	whose	king - dom
li - ving	God,____	whose	mer - cy
li - ving	God____	is	reign - ing—

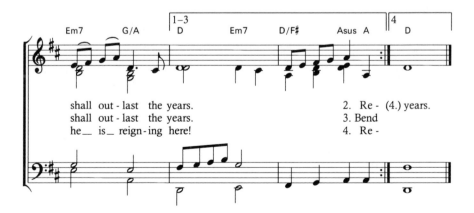

shall out - last the years.
shall out - last the years.
he__ is__ reign - ing here!

2. Re - (4.) years.
3. Bend
4. Re -

125 Sing praise to God

The vicar of Bray   87 87 D

English traditional melody
arr. Iona Community

Sing praise to God on mountain tops
and in earth's lowest places,
from blue lagoon to polar waste,
from ocean to oasis.
No random rock produced this world
but God's own will and wonder.
Thus hills rejoice and valleys sing
and clouds concur with thunder.

2　Sing praise to God where grasses grow
and flowers display their beauty,
where Nature weaves her myriad web
through love as much as duty.
The seasons in their cycle speak
of earth's complete provision.
Let nothing mock inherent good
nor treat it with derision.

3　Sing praise to God where fishes swim
and birds fly in formation,
where animals of every kind
diversify creation.
All life that finds its home on earth
is meant to be respected.
Let nothing threaten, for base ends,
what God through grace perfected.

4　Sing praise to God where humankind
its majesty embraces,
where different races, creeds and tongues
distinguish different faces.
God's image in each child of earth
shall never pale or perish.
So treat with love each human soul
and thus God's goodness cherish.

John Bell (b. 1949)
Graham Maule (b. 1958)

126 The kingdom of God

Paderborn 10 10 11 11

German traditional melody
from Paderborn Gesangbuch, 1765

Alternative tune: HANOVER, *Church Hymnary: Third Edition* no. 35; *Revised Church Hymnary* no. 9

The kingdom of God
is justice and joy,
for Jesus restores
what sin would destroy;
God's power and glory
in Jesus we know,
and here and hereafter
the kingdom shall grow.

2 The kingdom of God
is mercy and grace,
the prisoners are freed,
the sinners find place,
the outcast are welcomed
God's banquet to share,
and hope is awakened
in place of despair.

3 The kingdom of God
is challenge and choice,
believe the good news,
repent and rejoice!
His love for us sinners
brought Christ to his cross,
our crisis of judgement
for gain or for loss.

4 God's kingdom is come,
the gift and the goal,
in Jesus begun,
in heaven made whole;
the heirs of the kingdom
shall answer his call,
and all things cry 'Glory!'
to God all in all.

Bryn Rees (1911–83)

127 There's a spirit in the air

Lauds 77 77

John Wilson (1905–92)

Small notes are for the accompaniment only.

There's a spirit in the air,
telling Christians everywhere:
'Praise the love that Christ revealed,
living, working, in our world.'

2 Lose your shyness, find your tongue,
tell the world what God has done:
God in Christ has come to stay.
Live tomorrow's life today!

3 When believers break the bread,
when a hungry child is fed,
praise the love that Christ revealed,
living, working, in our world.

4 Still the Spirit gives us light,
seeing wrong and setting right:
God in Christ has come to stay.
Live tomorrow's life today!

5 When a stranger's not alone,
where the homeless find a home,
praise the love that Christ revealed,
living, working, in our world.

6 May the Spirit fill our praise,
guide our thoughts and change our ways.
God in Christ has come to stay.
Live tomorrow's life today!

7 There's a Spirit in the air,
calling people everywhere:
praise the love that Christ revealed,
living, working, in our world.

Brian Wren (b. 1936)

128 Who can sound the depths of sorrow

Have mercy, Lord

*Words and music
by Graham Kendrick (b. 1950)*

INTRODUCTION

Unison
VERSE

1. Who can

sound the depths of sor-row in the Fa-ther-heart of God, for the
(2.) scorned the truth you gave us, we have bowed to o-ther lords, we have

child-ren we've re-ject-ed, for the lives so deep-ly scarred? And each
sac-ri-ficed the child-ren on the al-tars of our gods. O let

light that we've ex-tin-guished has brought dark-ness to our land:
truth a-gain shine on us, let your ho-ly fear des-cend:

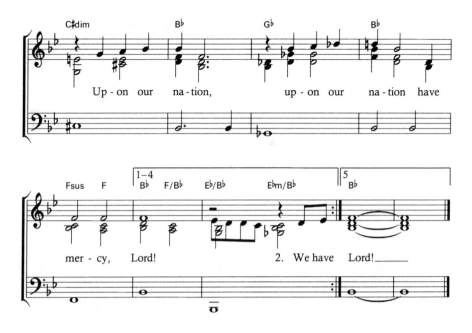

Up - on our na - tion, up - on our na - tion have

mer - cy, Lord! 2. We have Lord!

3 Who can stand before your anger;
who can face your piercing eyes?
For you love the weak and helpless,
and you hear the victims' cries.
Yes, you are a God of justice,
and your judgement surely comes:
Upon our nation, upon our nation
have mercy, Lord!

4 Who will stand against the violence?
Who will comfort those who mourn?
In an age of cruel rejection,
who will build for love a home?
Come and shake us into action,
come and melt our hearts of stone:
Upon your people, upon your people,
have mercy, Lord!

5 Who can sound the depths of mercy
in the Father-heart of God?
For there is a Man of sorrows
who for sinners shed his blood.
He can heal the wounds of nations,
he can wash the guilty clean:
Because of Jesus, because of Jesus
have mercy, Lord!

Graham Kendrick (b. 1950)

129 Think of a world without any flowers

Genesis

Graham Westcott (b. 1947)

1. Think of a world with - out_ a - ny flo - wers, think of a wood with - out_ a - ny trees, think of a sky with - out_ a - ny sun - shine, think of the air with - out_ a - ny breeze: we

A more elaborate version of the accompaniment (which can still be used with the instrumental descant) may be found on p. 265.

thank you, Lord, for flow'rs and trees and sun - shine; we

thank you, Lord, and praise your ho - ly name.

The rhythms in subsequent verses need to be adjusted slightly to fit the words.

PART 1

Think of a world without any flowers,
think of a wood without any trees,
think of a sky without any sunshine,
think of the air without any breeze:
we thank you, Lord, for flowers and trees and sunshine;
we thank you, Lord, and praise your holy name.

2 Think of a world without any animals,
think of a world without any herd,
think of a stream without any fishes,
think of a dawn without any bird:
we thank you, Lord, for all your living creatures;
we thank you, Lord, and praise your holy name.

PART 2

3 Think of a world without any paintings,
think of a room where all the walls are bare,
think of a rainbow without any colours,
think of the earth with darkness everywhere:
we thank you, Lord, for paintings and for colours;
we thank you, Lord, and praise your holy name.

4 Think of a world without any poetry,
think of a book without any words,
think of a song without any music,
think of a hymn without any verse:
we thank you, Lord, for poetry and music;
we thank you, Lord, and praise your holy name.

5 Think of a world without any science,
think of a journey with nothing to explore,
think of a quest without any mystery,
nothing to seek and nothing left in store:
we thank you, Lord, for miracles of science;
we thank you, Lord, and praise your holy name.

6 Think of a world without any people,
think of a street with no-one living there,
think of a town without any houses,
no-one to love and nobody to care:
we thank you, Lord, for families and friendships;
we thank you, Lord, and praise your holy name.

PART 3

7 Think of a world without any worship,
think of a God without his only Son,
think of a cross without a resurrection,
only a grave and not a victory won:
we thank you, Lord, for showing us our Saviour;
we thank you, Lord, and praise your holy name.

8 Thanks to our Lord for being here among us,
thanks be to him for sharing all we do,
thanks for our Church and all the love we find here,
thanks for this place and all its promise true:
we thank you, Lord, for life in all its richness;
we thank you, Lord, and praise your holy name.

Bunty Newport (b. 1927)

This song was designed to be sung at intervals during worship.
Appropriate verses should be selected for each occasion, or point in the service, always ending with v. 8.

GLORY TO GOD IN THE WORLD

Graham Westcott (b. 1947)
arr. Helen Killick (b. 1965)

ALTERNATIVE ACCOMPANIMENT

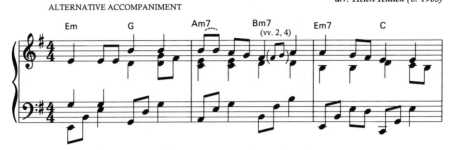

Index of select themes

Index of biblical references

Index of tunes and metres

Index of authors, translators, and sources of words

Index of composers, arrangers, and sources of music

An asterisk (*) indicates a harmonization, adaptation, or arrangement.

American traditional melody
34, 86(*i*)
Anchors' *Psalmody*, *c.*1721   41
Appleford, P. R. N.   53, 100,
121

Bach, J. S.   95(*i*)*, 104(*i*)*
Barnard, J.   8(*ii*), 56*, 62*, 76*,
80, 89*
Bateman, P.   91*
Baughen, M.   8(*i*), 21, 37, 47,
116
Beaumont, G.   74
Beethoven, L. van   28
Bell, J. L.   3, 48, 65, 68, 84*,
85, 88*, 93*, 97, 103*
Burt, P.   50

Carter, F. G.   69(*i*)
Carter, S.   60
Chinese melody   92
Clarke, J.   27
Coates, E.   11
Coates, K. W.   54
Coleman, T. B.   36
Collison, V.   67
Colvin, T.   84*, 115*
Converse, C.   69(*ii*)
Cooke, G.   82
Cutts, P.   77

Daniels, J.   109
Davies, W.   94
Davison, D.   38*, 98*, 120*
Dawn, M.   5
Dufford, B.   108

English traditional melody   32,
44, 57, 62, 125
Evans, D.   2

French traditional melody   20

Gardiner's *Sacred Melodies*, 1815
106
German traditional melody
126
Ghanaian traditional melody
115
Greatorex, W.   29
Green, H.   58
Green, M.   30

Handel, G. F.   31
Harvey, J.   114

Hassler, H. L.   104(*i*)
Himmels-Lust, 1679   95(*i*)
Hine, S.   23*
Holst, G.   22

Iliff, D.   7*, 102*, 116*
Inwood, P.   26*
Iona Community   52*, 112*,
125*
Irish traditional melody   89(*ii*),
104(*ii*)
Israeli traditional melody   81

Jackson, F.   110

Kendrick, G.   19, 55, 79, 91,
107, 118, 122, 124, 128
Killick, H.   1*, 2*, 14*, 16*,
27*, 34*, 42*, 48*, 50*, 57*,
90*, 105*, 108*, 129*

Larsson, J.   64
Loh, I.   92*
Lovelace, A. C.   86(*i*)*
Lunt, J.   39

Mansell, D.   15
Maries, A.   13, 39*
Martin, G.   99
Milner, A.   90
Monk, W. H.   66

Naylor, E. W.   78
Newport, W.   111
Nicaraguan melody   112
Norton, C.   109*
Nyberg, A.   71*, 101*
Nystrom, M.   35

Osborne, L.   96
Oxford University Press   49*,
70*, 104(*ii*)*, 115*

Paderborn Gesangbuch, 1765
126
Paris Antiphoner, 1681   7
Parker, H.   63
Parry, C. H.   4, 59
Parry, J.   43
Peacock, D.   124*
Philips, T.   17
Piae Cantiones, 1582   102

Reith, A.   81*
Rejoice and Sing, 1991   73*,
101*

Richards, N. & T.   1
Rosevear, H.   111*
Ruddle, V.   113
Runyon, W. M.   12

Sands, E.   26
Schutte, D. L.   49
Scottish traditional melody
24, 38, 70, 88, 98, 103, 105,
120
Shaw, M.   20*, 87, 117
Sheldon, R.   11*
Slater, G.   86(*ii*)
Smart, G. T.   33
Smart, H. T.   83, 119
Somervell, A.   123
South African traditional
melody   71, 101
Steiner, J. L.   40
Sullivan, A.   75
Swedish traditional melody   23
Swinstead, E. H.   46

Taylor, C. V.   10
Temple, S.   56
Terry, R.   45
Thomson, P.   109
Thornton, J.   37*
Traditional Malawian evening
hymn   93
Traditional North Malawian
melody   84
Trautwein, D.   73
Tredinnick, N.   8(*i*)*, 18, 21*

Urdu traditional melody   16

Vaughan Williams, R.   44*

Walker, C.   26*
Warren, N.   24*, 30*, 61, 81*,
95(*ii*)
Welsh traditional melody   76
Wesley, S. S.   51, 72
Westcott, G.   129
White, I.   14, 42
Williams, T. J.   9
Wilson, D.   25
Wilson, J.   127
Wonnacott, O.   6

Young-Soo, N.   52

273

Index of first lines and titles

Where titles differ from first lines, they are shown in *italic*.

274